ASSESSMENT
IN THE PRIMARY
CLASSROOM

Sara Miller McCune founded SAGE Publishing in 1965 to support the dissemination of usable knowledge and educate a global community. SAGE publishes more than 1000 journals and over 800 new books each year, spanning a wide range of subject areas. Our growing selection of library products includes archives, data, case studies and video. SAGE remains majority owned by our founder and after her lifetime will become owned by a charitable trust that secures the company's continued independence.

Los Angeles | London | New Delhi | Singapore | Washington DC | Melbourne

ASSESSMENT
IN THE PRIMARY
CLASSROOM

PRINCIPLES AND PRACTICE

SARAH EARLE

WITH

EMILY ASBURY, NIAMH MCGROGAN, DARREN MCKAY & LYNN SALTER

Learning Matters
An imprint of SAGE Publications Ltd
1 Oliver's Yard
55 City Road
London EC1Y 1SP

SAGE Publications Inc.
2455 Teller Road
Thousand Oaks, California 91320

SAGE Publications India Pvt Ltd
B 1/I 1 Mohan Cooperative Industrial Area
Mathura Road
New Delhi 110 044

SAGE Publications Asia-Pacific Pte Ltd
3 Church Street
#10-04 Samsung Hub
Singapore 049483

First published in 2019

Editor: Amy Thornton
Senior project editor: Chris Marke
Copy editor: Diana Chambers
Proofreader: Clare Weaver
Indexer: Anne Solamito
Marketing manager: Lorna Patkai
Cover design: Wendy Scott
Typeset by: C&M Digitals (P) Ltd, Chennai, India
Printed in the UK

Library of Congress Control Number: 2019935709

British Library Cataloguing in Publication Data

A catalogue record for this book is available from the British Library

ISBN 978-1-5264-4997-9
ISBN 978-1-5264-4998-6 (pbk)

At SAGE we take sustainability seriously. Most of our products are printed in the UK using responsibly sourced papers and boards. When we print overseas we ensure sustainable papers are used as measured by the PREPS grading system. We undertake an annual audit to monitor our sustainability.

CONTENTS

About the authors   vii

1   Introduction   1
Sarah Earle

2   Key terms   8
Sarah Earle, Darren McKay and Niamh McGrogan

3   Formative use of assessment by teachers   19
Lynn Salter and Sarah Earle

4   Formative use of assessment by pupils   33
Niamh McGrogan and Sarah Earle

5   Summative use of assessment   46
Darren McKay and Sarah Earle

6   Pupil progress and progression   58
Emily Asbury

7   Using data to support school improvement   73
Darren McKay

8   Moderation for professional learning   86
Sarah Earle and Tamsin Grimmer

9   Conclusion   97
Sarah Earle

Index   105

WHO IS THIS BOOK FOR?

Trainee teachers and those new to teaching.

Any teacher considering principles assessment for the first time.

All those who want to take a fresh look at assessment in primary schools.

School leadership staff responsible for changing practices across the school.

ABOUT THE AUTHORS

ABOUT THE AUTHOR

Dr Sarah Earle leads the Teacher Assessment in Primary Science (TAPS) project at Bath Spa University, working in collaboration with schools across the UK since 2013 to develop support for assessment. Prior to this, during her 13 years teaching in primary schools, she was assessment coordinator and science subject leader, before moving to initial teacher education as a Senior Lecturer for Primary PGCE at Bath Spa University in 2012. She gained a PhD in assessment in 2018 and supports teachers with assessment and primary science via online resources, publications and face-to-face professional learning. She is also a member of the Chartered Teacher Assessment Board, a Primary Science Quality Mark Senior Regional hub leader and Reviews Editor for the Association of Science Education's *Primary Science* journal.

CHAPTER AUTHORS

Emily Asbury is a Senior Lecturer in Primary English for the Institute of Education at Bath Spa University; she teaches on the PGCE and EYITT postgraduate teacher training routes, as well as teaching on undergraduate and TeachFirst routes. She also lectures in professional studies and supports CPD in primary schools. Alongside working as a primary school teacher and middle leader in South Gloucestershire, Emily completed a Master's in Education which explored gender gaps in primary writing attainment. She is currently working on a research project that investigates the representations of marginalised groups in children's books. Her research interests include equality in educational attainment and international perspectives on reading and early literacy, alongside participatory research methodologies.

Tamsin Grimmer teaches on the Early Years Initial Teacher Training PGCE Programme at Bath Spa University. She has a wealth of experience supporting Early Years teachers and educators in all aspects of their provision, including formative and summative assessment. As a consultant and trainer, she has improved outcomes for children and families, working as an Early Years Consultant for two local authorities, and managed the implementation of the Early Years Foundation Stage Profile and moderation processes. She has written two books aimed at practitioners and her third on superhero play will be released later this year. Tamsin also puts theory into practice with her three young children, keeping her feet firmly on the ground.

Niamh McGrogan is a Senior Lecturer in Mathematics for the Institute for Education at Bath Spa University. As Head of Year and Maths Lead in a large Kent primary school, her responsibilities included the design and implementation of an alternative approach to whole-school assessment following the introduction of the 2014 curriculum and assessment without levels. She obtained her Master's degree with the Open University before progressing to an academic career at Bath Spa University. As 'Teachers as Researchers' module lead on the PGCE, she works closely with colleagues to support students' understanding of how children learn, and the use of assessment for learning in both theory and practice. She is passionate about supporting teachers in engaging with and in research, and collaborates with both students and school teachers to conduct research in the classroom and draw conclusions that can enhance the development and understanding of practice. Her current doctoral research investigates research capacity building in primary schools through such collaborative research activity.

Darren McKay has been a Professional Studies Senior Lecturer in Primary ITE since 2014, currently working at Bath Spa University. He has over two decades of experience working in primary schools with 14 years' experience as a Senior Leader. He has been the assessment lead in several primary schools and worked as a consultant supporting school leaders develop assessment procedures in England and South Wales. As the Professional Studies Module Leader for the BEd and PGCE at Middlesex University, he worked closely with trainees, school mentors and university colleagues to develop an understanding of assessment practices in schools and the impact they have on children's progress.

Lynn Salter is Senior Lecturer on Bath Spa University's Primary and Early Years PGCE where she leads the Professional Studies strand, lectures in maths and developed the primary Behaviour Specialism. She underpins her work in initial teacher education with 18 years of teaching experience spanning the Early Years, primary and secondary age range, gained in both the UK and USA. As a senior school leader, she has led curriculum and assessment, working on projects with both Wiltshire Local Authority and the National College of Teaching aimed at narrowing the gap for pupils vulnerable to underachievement. Prior to teaching, she worked as an international training and development consultant, with one of her specialist areas being workplace equality and diversity.

1

INTRODUCTION

SARAH EARLE

PURPOSE OF THIS CHAPTER

In this chapter we will:

- explain the importance of assessment for teaching in the primary school;
- consider the many purposes and implications of assessment;
- introduce the book and its chapters.

WHO IS THIS BOOK FOR?

This book provides an introduction to assessment in the primary school. It is aimed at any in the teaching profession who are either considering principled assessment for the first time or those who would like to take a fresh look at the assessment practices in their school. Thus, it will be useful for both those new to teaching and those who are responsible for changing practices across the school. Examples are largely drawn from England and Wales, but the principles explored in this book are relevant to any context.

It is easy to get used to a system, assume that the status quo must continue because that is 'how it has always been'. However, educational norms can change and what once felt essential can be re-evaluated to decide on its necessity. For example, the growth of the accountability system in England led to a concern to evidence learning, with extensive marking policies becoming the norm. This led to such practices as 'triple marking' whereby teachers would respond to pupils' responses to their marking. Practices such as triple marking and frequent collection of assessment data ('data drops') built over time into the expected norm, rather than an occasional strategy, which made the system unmanageable, sparking calls for workload reduction (Teacher Workload Advisory Group, 2018). The place of marking will be explored further in Chapter 3; suffice to say that many schools are now rewriting their marking policies to become 'feedback policies' that focus on the purpose of the interaction, rather than the colour of the pen.

WHY IS AN UNDERSTANDING OF ASSESSMENT IMPORTANT?

Assessment is a powerful driver in education: it influences school and classroom culture; it determines what is taught and how; and it directly impacts on pupil and teacher conceptualisations of learning (Edwards, 2013). Assessment is a complex, embedded and integral part of teaching with a multitude of strategies, purposes and consequences. As pupil experience is shaped by assessment practices, it is essential for such practices to be well understood.

It can be tempting to feel that there is no need to make decisions about assessment because we just have to 'do what we are told'. However, underlying this 'gut-feeling' is the assumption that assessment is summative, that its sole purpose is for summarising attainment and comparing pupils in a standardised way, which will be spelled out to us in statutory guidelines. However, this is only a small part of the assessment story. Assessment also includes the non-statutory school processes; the end of topic checks; the start of topic elicitation activities; the conversations with parents or senior leaders or pupils; the tweaks to the next or current lesson in response to feedback from pupils. In short, assessment is a key part of the teaching and learning cycle, as represented in Figure 1.1.

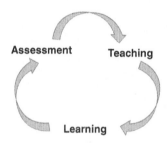

Assessment   Teaching

Learning

Figure 1.1   The teaching, learning and assessment cycle

Figure 1.1 is a common way of representing the relationship between teaching, learning and assessment, demonstrating the importance of all three. This can be understood at a micro level, within the lesson, or at a macro level, from lesson to lesson or term to term. Embedded in the representation is also the way that assessment can both inform teaching (formative) and can summarise learning (summative), since the teacher could start with an assessment to help them to plan their teaching or end with an assessment to check on the learning that has taken place. However, it also appears to suggest a neat order and separation of actions, which does not capture the 'messiness' of classroom teaching. Figure 1.2 proposes an alternative representation, which shows the multiple places for assessment within the teaching and learning cycle.

Figure 1.2 provides more detail on the different roles of assessment in the teaching and learning cycle. The diagram highlights that formative assessment can take place both within and between lessons, with on-the-spot adjustments to teaching within the lesson and longer term adjustments to planning for the next lessons. The assessment becomes formative when the information is used to support future learning, as will be discussed further in Chapter 2, when we consider assessment terminology in more detail. The summative role of assessment is also noted in Figure 1.2, where assessment is used to summarise attainment at a particular point in time. As with all diagrams, the

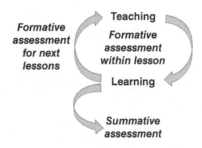

Figure 1.2   Assessment in the teaching and learning cycle

representation is a simplification because learning experiences cannot be categorised so neatly in practice; however, the aim was to draw attention to the multiple roles of assessment, which will be explored more fully in the rest of the book.

Having established that assessment is an integral part of teaching and learning, it is easier to justify the importance of understanding its principles, so that informed decisions can be made about practice in the classroom. Teachers' understanding and application of assessment is sometimes referred to as 'assessment literacy'. Klenowski and Wyatt-Smith (2014) assert that high-quality assessment requires teachers to have well developed *assessment literacy* (p1), an understanding of assessment, which will be a recurring theme throughout the book. Assessment practice will represent a complex mix of assessment knowledge and priorities at an individual, school and national level. DeLuca and Johnson (2017) note that, despite widespread recognition of the need for assessment literate teachers, research has indicated a low level of assessment knowledge in the teaching profession (p121), hence the need for texts like this one.

Understanding and application of assessment is a requirement for qualification as a teacher. Table 1.1 contains extracts from the teachers' standards documents from across the UK. Each discuss the use of assessment as an essential part of the qualification to become, and continue to be, a teacher.

Table 1.1   Assessment descriptors from teachers' standards requirements across the UK

Country	Descriptor
England	6. Make accurate and productive use of assessment: • know and understand how to assess the relevant subject and curriculum areas, including statutory assessment requirements; • make use of formative and summative assessment to secure pupils' progress; • use relevant data to monitor progress, set targets, and plan subsequent lessons; • give pupils regular feedback, both orally and through accurate marking, and encourage pupils to respond to the feedback. Department for Education (2011, p12)

(Continued)

Table 1.1 (Continued)

Country	Descriptor
Scotland	3.3. Pupil assessment: use assessment, recording and reporting as an integral part of the teaching process to support and enhance learning. Registered teachers: • systematically develop and use an extensive range of strategies, approaches and associated materials for formative and summative assessment purposes, appropriate to the needs of all learners and the requirements of the curriculum and awarding and accrediting bodies; • enable all learners to engage in self evaluation and peer assessment to benefit learning; • record assessment information in a systematic and meaningful way in order to enhance teaching and learning and fulfil the requirements of the curriculum and awarding bodies; • use the results of assessment to identify development needs at class, group and individual level and as a basis for dialogue with learners about their progress and targets; • produce clear and informed reports for parents and other agencies which discuss learners' progress and matters related to personal, social and emotional development in a sensitive and constructive way. General Teaching Council for Scotland (2012, p17)
Northern Ireland	Teachers will: • focus on assessment for learning by monitoring pupils' progress, giving constructive feedback to help pupils reflect on and improve their learning; • select from a range of assessment strategies to evaluate pupils' learning, and use this information in their planning to help make their teaching more effective; • assess the levels of pupils' attainment against relevant benchmarking data and understand the relationship between pupil assessment and target setting; • liaise orally and in written reports in an effective manner with parents or carers on their child's progress and achievements. General Teaching Council for Northern Ireland (2011, p17)
Wales	The teacher consistently secures the best outcomes for learners through progressively refining teaching, influencing learners and advancing learning. Assessment: • Newly qualified: The range of purposes and practices for assessment is understood and articulated. • Induction: Assessment is used effectively to pinpoint learning needs for all learners. • Highly effective practitioner: Specialised assessment techniques are employed for identified learners and there is a commitment to working with colleagues and other agencies to best meet identified needs. Welsh Government (2017, p24)

Assessment literacy applies to all stages of a teacher's career and all areas of the curriculum. The teacher standards in Table 1.1 clearly link assessment to pupil progress; assessment is a tool for planning for and developing experiences that will enhance learning.

PLACING ASSESSMENT IN CONTEXT

Assessment is fundamental to the practice of education; it is not neutral, but is value-laden. It influences both the teaching and those being taught: *assessment does not objectively measure what is already there, but rather creates and shapes what is measured* (Stobart, 2008, p1). Assessment processes determine what is *valuable to learn* and what success will look like. If the judgement at the end of the year is only based on part of the curriculum, then it is that part of the curriculum that will become the focus for teaching.

The functions and effect of assessment have received much attention, with some arguing (e.g. Black and Wiliam, 1998) that assessment should have an impact on learning, otherwise there is little point in conducting the assessment in the first place. Research into formative assessment champions the use of assessment to support learners with their next steps (Gardner et al., 2010), while summative assessment became viewed in a negative light because of suggestions that it was the cause of curriculum narrowing and teaching to the test (Harlen, 2013). However, education systems require both purposes to be fulfilled, with assessment information used both to support learning and to summarise achievements for a range of audiences such as pupils, parents, senior leaders and the next class teacher.

The competing uses of assessment places the teacher in a *conflicted position*, with assessment for accountability seeming to require a different approach to using assessment as part of the learning process (Green and Oates, 2009, p233). Lum (2015) suggests that there has been a recent *paradigm shift*, a change in views about what assessment is for. In the past, the primary aim of assessment was to compare students against each other, to rank them in order to make decisions about schools, sets, final grades and ultimately jobs. IQ tests, entrance exams and the like were all designed to identify the student's place in society. This comparison purpose still exists, but more recently there has been a move to refocus assessment so that it also supports learning, to focus on the progress of the individual. Assumptions about pre-designated outcomes are being questioned, with initiatives designed to support access and raise expectations. Understanding this change in the perception of assessment may not make the teacher's job any easier, but it does help us to realise the importance of considering the purposes of our classroom assessments.

Assessment has increasingly become a political issue, with international comparison of student achievement data leading governments to implement assessment reforms and standards-driven curricula (Connelly et al., 2012, p593). For example, in England the Task Group on Assessment and Testing (TGAT; DES, 1988) 'levels' structure was removed and replaced by a system based on age-related expectations in 2014 (DfE, 2013). After using level descriptors for 25 years, there were suggestions that the system was leading to the unhelpful labelling of children and teaching to the 'test' since schools were held accountable for results. Together with this, there had been a change in perception of the TGAT level 4, which had begun as a pupil average, but had become a target for all (Whetton, 2009). The move from level descriptors to age-related judgements was seen as a radical shift for schools, with the Commission on Assessment without Levels (2015) noting that *the system has been so conditioned by levels that there is considerable challenge in moving away from them . . . [with]*

some schools trying to recreate levels based on the new national curriculum (p4). It is taking some time for valid, reliable and manageable systems of assessment to emerge, especially since schools were encouraged to develop their own systems with little guidance.

IN THIS BOOK

Assessment is an area full of terminology, thus Chapter 2 will focus on untangling and defining the key terms that will be used throughout the rest of the book: assessment, formative, summative, validity, reliability, attainment, progress and achievement.

Formative assessment, which is designed to support learning, has been spread across two chapters, in order to facilitate discussion from different viewpoints. Chapter 3 will consider the role of the teacher in using and applying formative assessment, exploring its use in planning and responsive teaching, together with a range of approaches, including the use of questioning, giving feedback, learning intentions and success criteria. Chapter 4 considers the role of the pupil in formative assessment and how they can be actively involved through processes such as self- and peer assessment.

Chapter 5 considers the summative use of assessment, with examples of strategies and statutory assessment, together with the use of the outcomes for reporting to a range of audiences. Chapter 6 looks at pupil progress in the classroom, with examples of ways to evidence the progression. Chapter 7 focuses on the use of data, considering pupil progress from a whole-school perspective.

Chapter 8 discusses moderation practices and considers how such experiences can be fruitful opportunities for professional learning. Chapter 9 draws together key messages to conclude the book.

Examples are used throughout to support the text to be both accessible and to challenge our thinking, by showing that there is a variety of practices that can share similar underpinning principles of assessment in the primary classroom.

REFERENCES

Black, P and Wiliam, D (1998) *Inside the Black Box*. London: GL Assessment.

Commission on Assessment without Levels (2015) *Final Report of the Commission on Assessment without Levels*. London: DfE.

Connolly, S, Klenowski, V and Wyatt-Smith, C (2012) Moderation and consistency of teacher judgement: teachers' views. *British Educational Research Journal*, 38(4): 593–614.

DeLuca, C and Johnson, S (2017) Developing assessment capable teachers in this age of accountability. *Assessment in Education: Principles, Policy & Practice*, 24(2): 121–6.

Department for Education (DfE) (2011) *Teachers' Standards*. London: DfE.

Department for Education (DfE) (2013) *National Curriculum in England*. London: DfE.

Department of Education and Science (DES) (1988) *National Curriculum Task Group on Assessment and Testing (TGAT): A Report*. London: Department of Education and Science and the Welsh Office.

Edwards, F (2013) Quality assessment by science teachers: five focus areas. *Science Education International,* *24*(2): 212–26.

Gardner, J, Harlen, W, Hayward, L, Stobart, G, with Montgomery, M (2010) *Developing Teacher Assessment.* Maidenhead: Open University Press.

General Teaching Council for Northern Ireland (2011) *Teaching: The Reflective Profession.* Belast: GTCNI.

General Teaching Council for Scotland (2012) *The Standards for Registration: Mandatory Requirements for Registration with the General Teaching Council for Scotland.* Edinburgh: GTC Scotland.

Green, S and Oates, T (2009) Considering the alternatives to national assessment arrangements in England: possibilities and opportunities. *Educational Research, 51*(2): 229–45.

Harlen, W (2013) *Assessment and Inquiry-based Science Education: Issues in Policy and Practice.* Trieste: Global Network of Science Academies.

Klenowski, V and Wyatt-Smith, C (2014) *Assessment for Education.* London: SAGE.

Lum, G (2015) Introduction, Afterword. In Davis, A and Winch, C, with Lum, G (eds) (2015) *Educational Assessment on Trial.* London: Bloomsbury.

Stobart, G. (2008) *Testing Times: The Uses and Abuses of Assessment.* London: Routledge.

Teacher Workload Advisory Group (2018) *Making Data Work: Report of the Teacher Workload Advisory Group.* London: DfE.

Welsh Government (2017) *Professional Standards for Teaching and Leadership.* Cardiff: Welsh Government.

Whetton, C (2009) A brief history of a testing time: national curriculum assessment in England 1989–2008. *Educational Research, 51*(2): 137–59.

2
KEY TERMS

SARAH EARLE, DARREN MCKAY AND NIAMH MCGROGAN

PURPOSE OF THIS CHAPTER

In this chapter, we will explore the following key terminology for primary assessment:

- formative and summative assessment;
- validity and reliability;
- attainment, progress and achievement.

INTRODUCTION

This chapter is designed to be a point of reference for use when reading the rest of the book, and when selecting, designing and interpreting assessments in the future. In order to unpick the key terminology in assessment, we draw on a wider range of literature than in other chapters, to develop a deeper understanding of the concepts and principles on which this book is based. It can be hard to step back from the detail of everyday practice, but a consideration of assessment principles can help to decide whether such practices are serving their purpose as well as they could.

In this chapter, we will define key terminology for assessment in primary schools. Nevertheless, it is important to note that teachers, school leaders, policy-makers and researchers may not all share the same meaning for these terms. Over time, the meaning of such words develops and so it is important to clarify what individuals understand by such terms in order to discuss them in practice.

We will begin by defining 'assessment' itself, before moving on to classic distinctions between formative and summative assessment and then to the key assessment principles of validity and reliability. The chapter will also include context-specific discussions, drawing on examples from Northern Ireland to consider diagnostic and evaluative assessment, and England to consider attainment, progress and achievement. Other context-specific examples can be found throughout the book – for example, a Welsh perspective can be found in Chapter 7, and Early Years is discussed in more detail in Chapters 6 and 8.

ASSESSMENT

Assessment is such a commonly used term that it is easy to assume that we all mean the same thing when we use the word. However, quite clear distinctions can be drawn between different conceptualisations of assessment; of particular interest is whether assessment is viewed as an object or a process. Consider for yourself: when you hear the word 'assessment', do you think of a particular task, like a test paper, or do you think of an ongoing process of making judgements as part of the lesson? Also, who is making those judgements? Is assessment only done by the teacher or can pupils be assessors too? Such unpicking of our understanding of assessment is necessary to be able to hold meaningful discussions in school.

For many practitioners, 'assessment' has become the shorthand for a 'thing' that happens at the end of term; however, in this book the term will be used more broadly. Assessment is seen as an integral part of teaching, the part where a judgement is made regarding learning. Such a judgement could be happening during or after the lesson, at any point during the sequence of lessons. Assessment includes the process of collecting and interpreting evidence to make judgements about pupil achievement (Harlen, 2007, p11). Again, a broad view of evidence is taken in this book; such evidence could include observation, dialogue, pupil recording, model-making, presentations, quizzes, posters, and so on. This evidence could be produced as part of normal classroom activities or be the result of a special task designed to elicit pupil explanations for the purposes of judging their attainment at a particular point in time. By using this broad view of assessment and evidence, all interactions with pupils potentially provide information that could support the teacher to make judgements. However, this is not to say that every interaction is a formal assessment task; assessment is seen as a process, not a set of stand-alone tasks.

Since assessment is about making judgements, it is important to identify the reference point, the criteria against which you are making the judgement. Three assessment terms are useful here (Gipps, 1994):

* Judgement against a previous performance is called ipsative.

* Judgement compared to peers is called norm-referenced.

* Judgement against a set of criteria like the National Curriculum is called criterion-referenced.

All three can be seen in schools – for example, checking whether a spelling test score is higher than last week (ipsative); deciding on groupings (norm-referenced); and deciding whether pupils have met the Age Related Expectation (ARE) for their National Curriculum year group (criterion-referenced). The latter is currently the most important in English schools since ARE is used for statutory judgements, but information related to previous performance is also useful – for example, when discussing progress with parents or senior leaders. In addition, comparing outcomes across the class or year group is an effective way of developing understanding of what ARE 'looks like', as will be discussed in Chapter 8.

FORMATIVE AND SUMMATIVE ASSESSMENT

A popular way to classify assessment is to make a distinction between formative and summative assessment, with the first focusing on learning and the second focusing on summarising attainment. This section will explore both types of assessment and clarify that it is the purpose and uses of the assessment that define it as formative or summative.

After Black and Wiliam reviewed assessment research in 1998, the Assessment Reform Group (ARG) argued that 'Assessment *of* Learning' (AoL), for the purposes of grading and reporting, should be considered separately to 'Assessment *for* Learning' (AfL), whose purpose was to support learning (ARG, 1999). The new terminology represented a call for *different priorities, new procedures and a new commitment*, after *too much attention being given to finding reliable ways of comparing children, teachers and schools* (ARG, 1999, p2). The aim of using the new term of 'AfL', which contained the word 'learning', was to emphasise the requirement to have an impact on learning, and AfL became a popular way to refer to formative assessment. Such a 'rebranding' was about shifting practitioner and policy focus, rather than the creation of new assessment concepts; the terms 'formative' and 'AfL', or 'summative' and 'AoL', are largely used interchangeably. Many authors have more recently returned to using 'formative' and 'summative', perhaps due to the perceived misunderstanding that 'AfL' could imply frequent testing (Mansell et al., 2009).

The purpose of *formative assessment* is to seek out and respond to information to enhance ongoing learning (Klenowski, 2009). It is an ongoing and planned part of classroom practice, where the teacher or pupil checks their progress and considers what to do next. The process is an integral part of teaching and learning, providing feedback for both the teacher and the pupils. Some refer to the elicitation of pupil understanding at the beginning of a topic as 'diagnostic' (see Box 2.1). AfL requires the active involvement of children, and researchers stress the importance of dialogue and questioning (Black and Harrison, 2010). Strategies associated with formative assessment include identifying and making explicit success criteria; elicitation of children's existing ideas; feedback; self-assessment and peer assessment (Wiliam, 2018), all of which will be discussed further in Chapters 3 and 4.

Black and Wiliam suggest that *assessment provides information to be used as feedback . . . Such assessment becomes 'formative assessment' when the evidence is actually used to adapt the teaching work to meet the needs* (1998, p2); thus, it is the use of assessment information to support the learning process that distinguishes formative and summative assessment, rather than the assessment task itself. The same task can be used formatively to decide on the focus for the next activity, or summatively to provide information about attainment at that point in time.

The purpose of *summative assessment* is to report or summarise attainment – for example, a report for parents or an end of topic activity that is designed to encapsulate what the pupil has learnt that term. For some, summative assessment is synonymous with testing. However, the term should be seen more broadly, particularly in primary education where accessibility is a significant issue for young children. Summative assessment can be based on a 'snapshot', an activity at a particular point in time, or it can be a 'summary' that takes a range of information into account. Both snapshot and summary assessments can take the form of grades or a narrative – for example, a description of what has been achieved to 'meet' an age-related expectation. A summary teacher judgement against the Levels of Progression (CCEA, 2017) in communication, mathematics and ICT in Northern Ireland, where there is no statutory summative testing at the end of primary school, considers both within and beyond subject-specific learning situations, with results validated through internal and external moderation processes.

Such summaries of learning can be reported to parents, other teachers, school leadership teams or school inspectors. In some cases, summative assessment is used to hold schools to account, with results becoming 'high stakes' when they are used for target setting and the ranking of schools. Some teachers may view formative assessment as 'good' and summative assessment as 'bad' (Harlen, 2013). This is because researchers describe the positive impact of formative assessment on children's learning (e.g. Hattie, 2009; Gardner et al., 2010), compared to findings of the harmful effects of high-stakes summative testing (Newton, 2009) and its distorting effects on the taught curriculum (Wiliam, 2003). However, schools require both purposes to be fulfilled, to support and summarise learning, so teachers need to consider purposes carefully when planning classroom assessments, taking into account consideration of the key principles of validity and reliability, which will be considered later in the chapter.

▬ BOX 2.1 ASSESSMENT TERMS IN NORTHERN IRELAND ▬

While the concepts that underpin the terms used in this chapter are consistent throughout the UK, the practice of implementing these can vary, and one example of this is assessment practice in Northern Ireland. In addition to formative and summative, the terms 'diagnostic assessment' and 'evaluative assessment' are used to define assessment processes.

Diagnostic assessment in Northern Ireland is defined by the Council for the Curriculum, Examinations and Assessment (CCEA, 2013) as the process by which teachers identify pupils' strengths and learning needs, usually at the beginning of a programme of learning. Similar to elicitation, the purpose is to examine the pupils' existing learning and determine how best to build on this through lessons and other learning activities.

Computer-based Assessment (CBA), a computerised test that produces a standardised score, is used in many schools to gain an understanding of pupil learning and areas for development. Diagnostic assessment is used at key points in the school year, usually early and at a mid-point in the year. Early in the year, the outcomes are used to identify those pupils in need of additional support, to inform classroom groupings and help support teachers' judgement of pupil learning. Tests used at the mid-point of the year support a review of progress and begin to inform diagnostic indications for the following year, as well as supporting judgements about pupil progress over the longer term.

Evaluative assessment seeks to inform *curriculum planning and provides information for monitoring and accountability* (CCEA, 2013). It draws from a range of quantitative and qualitative data including:

- relevant school policy documents;

- class schemes of work for Areas of Learning;

- guidance materials;

- assessment resources;

- pupil information on progress and performance (including samples of pupil work).

(CCEA, 2013)

The outcomes of evaluative assessment are shared to enable schools to develop and refine action plans, supporting teachers to set broader class targets to support individual pupil progress.

ATTAINMENT, PROGRESS AND ACHIEVEMENT IN ENGLAND

'Attainment' and 'progress' are terms that have been used in schools for many years and, in our experience, there seems to be a shared understanding between school staff and Ofsted about what each means. Put simply, 'attainment' is an outcome at a specific point and 'progress' is the measure of improvement made over time. The example in Box 2.2 illustrates this.

BOX 2.2 AN EXAMPLE TO ILLUSTRATE ATTAINMENT AND PROGRESS

Child A takes a test to measure how many phonemes they can read on entering a class at age 4. They score 10. At the end of the school year, they are tested to see how many phonemes they can read and they score 38. The child's attainment at the start of the year is recorded as 10 and at the end of the year as 38. As they can read 28 more phonemes at the end of the year when compared to the start of the year, their progress is 28 more phonemes. Often this information is recorded in a table using a spreadsheet or mark book.

Number of phonemes accurately read by child A

Score at start of year	10	attainment
Score at end of year	38	attainment
Progress	+28	progress

Both attainment and progress can be used to make judgements about how a child, teacher and school are performing in comparison to other individual children in the class, the class mean result, other schools and the nationally expected standard. When comparing the attainment of child A (Box 2.2) to the other children in the class and to the performance of other children in the school or nationally, a norm-referenced judgement is being made. When calculating the progress made, an ipsative judgement is being made. To make a criterion-referenced judgement, we would need to compare child A's attainment and progress to the expected attainment and progress as set out in a set of criteria – for example, by the school or DfE. This could be recorded in a table, as shown in Box 2.3 (which only contains data from three children for simplicity).

BOX 2.3 AN EXAMPLE TO ILLUSTRATE CLASS ANALYSIS FOR ATTAINMENT AND PROGRESS

Number of phonemes accurately read by children in class R against school's criteria

	Child A	Child J	Child X	Mean for class	
Score at start of year	10^	30*	24	15	attainment
Score at end of year	38^	44	44	40	attainment
Progress	+28*	+14^	+20	+25	progress

Key: above expected*; at expected; below expected^

Using this data, a simple analysis can be completed, as follows.

- The attainment at the end of the year was lower for child A than child J and X.
- The progress made by child A was greater than child J and X. The progress made by child A was greater than the mean progress of the class.

Questions to consider

If the highest score possible on the test was 44, what does the data tell you about the progress and attainment of child J and child X?

How confident are you in your conclusions based on this one score?

Achievement is a less straightforward term. The *Oxford English Dictionary* (2018) defines achievement as *the action of achieving something; completion, accomplishment, successful execution.* You would be forgiven for thinking that this definition is similar to attainment. If you were to use a thesaurus to find a synonym for attainment, achievement is almost always listed. However, attainment and achievement have come to mean two different things in today's schools in England. In the UK government's initiative, *Every Child Matters* (HMSO, 2003), both the terms 'attainment' and 'achievement' were being used to describe an outcome, e.g. GCSE grades. In subsequent years, Ofsted inspectors started asking schools about the attainment, progress and achievement of the children. Achievement and attainment had become two distinct phenomena. 'Achievement' was being used to define the combination of 'attainment' and 'progress'. The *School Inspection Handbook* (Ofsted, 2018a) states:

> In judging achievement, inspectors will give most weight to pupils' progress. This will be achieved by scrutinising children's work, observing parts of lessons, talking to children, talking to staff, analysing national data and the school's own data. By triangulating this information, inspectors will make a judgement about the progress children are making towards meeting or exceeding the expected attainment for their age . . .

> (p58)

The *Ofsted Inspection – Clarification for Schools* document (Ofsted, 2018b, p3) clearly states that Ofsted does not require that primary schools record children's achievement. This is in line with the recommendations made by the committee led by John McIntosh, *Final Report on the Commission on Assessment without Levels* (2015), and the UK government's response (STA, 2015). How schools have risen to these challenges is covered in the subsequent chapters of this book.

KEY ASSESSMENT PRINCIPLES OF VALIDITY AND RELIABILITY

It is easy to get lost in the detail of individual assessment results when analysing pupil outcomes – for example, making the assumption that Child J and Child X (Box 2.3) are of the same 'ability' because they received the same score in a phoneme test. However, it is important to stand back and consider the key principles of validity and reliability for classroom assessments, so that we can decide whether they merit the conclusions we are drawing from them.

VALIDITY

Validity concerns whether an assessment is actually assessing what it claims to and the extent to which it is fit for purpose (Green and Oates, 2009). It is a multifaceted concept and its key aspects will be explored in this section. Validity is primarily about purposes – for example, if the purpose of formative assessment is to stimulate further learning, then the assessment will only be valid if further learning is supported (Stobart, 2012). Since it is about purposes and uses, validity is not a 'static property' of an assessment, which is either there or not; validity is an ongoing consideration when planning and implementing assessment practices.

Both *content* and *construct validity* insist that the assessment measures what it is meant to – the conceptual content and the skills for a particular subject. Content validity concerns how well the agreed curriculum is sampled, while construct validity concerns how well this represents the underlying skill or concept (Stobart, 2009). For example, in the case of mathematics, a multiplication tables test would not validly assess the full range of mathematical concepts; however, it could be combined with other assessments to provide a fuller picture of pupil performance.

An important consideration is the 'sampling' of the construct, which bit of the subject is assessed. The assessment will consider a sample of the subject matter in a particular context or particular format. It is not measuring the construct directly; assessment is an approximation. Nevertheless, what is sampled can affect both the validity of the assessment and the teaching of the subject. Messick (1989) suggests that the best protection against invalid assessment inferences is to minimise construct under-representation and construct-irrelevant variance. *Construct under-representation* concerns how much of the subject matter is assessed – for example, if only the decoding of words is assessed for reading, comprehension of the text will be under-represented. To avoid *construct-irrelevance*, a focus on the subject is required – for example, a teacher marking pupil work in history may comment on the neatness of handwriting or use of grammar, thus assessing writing skills rather than historical enquiry skills.

Predictive validity requires the assessment to provide accurate predictions for the outcomes of future assessments (Isaacs et al., 2013, p137). This has arguably become more important in primary schools as teachers have increasingly been asked to predict the performance of children at the end of the year or Key Stage on the basis of 'mock' tests, a practice that is questioned by many. Under a numerical or levelling system, this prediction or target could be worked out via a formula – for example, moving up two-thirds of a level per year. Such use of assessments appears to rely on dubious assumptions: that learning is linear, with children moving in a predictable way along the continuum each year (Stobart, 2008). Alternatively, the assumption could be made that the assessment is measuring some underlying 'ability' within the child which will remain stable as they move through school; such innate fixed intelligence remains a topic of fierce debate in education circles. Unfortunately, there is not space to discuss it here, but suffice to say that Stobart (2009) warns of over-simplistic interpretations of assessments that treat the result as a direct measure of an underlying educational standard (p175).

RELIABILITY

Reliability concerns trust in the accuracy or consistency of an assessment (Mansell et al., 2009) – for example, whether the same result would be found if the task was given on a different occasion or marked by a different teacher. Reliability can be internal, within the assessment such as the wording of questions and the conditions under which they are taken, or external, between assessments such as consistency in application of marking criteria. In order to be valid, an assessment needs to reliably assess what it has been designed to, so reliability is a necessary condition of validity, but it is not sufficient, since to be valid an assessment also needs to sample enough of the subject content.

Inter-rater reliability addresses whether the same judgement would be made by different teachers on the basis of the same set of evidence. This requires a judgement against a reference point, a previous performance (ipsative), a peer (norm-referenced) or a set of criteria like the National Curriculum (criterion-referenced), as noted above. Agreement between markers through standardisation and moderation will be discussed in Chapter 8. Where inter-rater reliability is deemed important – for example, when comparing end of Key Stage results – the criteria are likely to be tightly specified. Such tight specification supports markers to agree on the grading of pupil outcomes, but also narrows the field of what is acceptable, calling the validity of the assessment into question if it is supposed to be assessing a broad sample of subject content. In addition, 'criteria compliance' can follow when objectives are too detailed, leading to surface-level ticking of a large number of criteria rather than in-depth learning: a 'tick-box culture' (Mansell et al., 2009). For example, concerns regarding the reliability of English writing assessments have led to the removal of KS2 writing SATs and complaints about the detailed list of objectives that should be ticked off for teacher assessment. New methods of 'comparative judgement' are being explored – for example, by www.nomoremarking.com – as a holistic alternative to criteria lists.

Assessment with the sole purpose of formatively supporting the pupil with their next steps would arguably be less concerned with reliability (Harlen, 2007), since comparison with others is not the prime purpose and the pupil is likely to have moved on in their learning before another 'rater' attempts to assess their learning. However, a shared understanding of criteria and 'what a good one looks like' supports both formative and summative assessment. Filer and Pollard (2000) caution that since school assessment necessarily takes place in a social context, the presumed 'objectivity' of assessment is actually a myth: no assessment can be perfectly objective, repeatable and reliable.

BALANCING VALIDITY AND RELIABILITY

Wiliam (2003) argues that there is inevitably a 'trade-off' between reliability and validity since reliability relies on a narrowing the task to help markers agree, while validity depends on the opposite: as broad a sampling of the subject as possible. Pollard utilises the broader term of 'dependability', which refers to the confidence placed in the assessment: *it reflects the outcomes of the struggle to achieve validity and reliability* (Pollard, 2014, p385). Mansell et al. (2009) suggest that the notion of 'dependability' includes consideration of both 'maximum validity' and 'optimal reliability' (p12).

One of the difficulties in assessment appears to be the balancing act between valid assessment of a whole detailed curriculum, while at the same time maintaining reliable, consistent judgements: Wiliam's (2003) 'trade-off'. Harlen (2007, p23) states: *an assessment cannot have both high validity and high reliability*; it is not possible to have highly repeatable, standardised assessment that samples the whole of the subject. Many argue that teacher assessment signifies a balance between the demands of reliability and validity, as represented in Figure 2.1, because it can be based on the wide range of evidence available to teachers in the classroom – for example, observations, discussions and practical activities (Gardner et al., 2010). With a collection of evidence and effective moderation procedures, where teachers compare and discuss judgements, Harlen (2007) argues that reliability of summative teacher assessment can be as high as it needs to be: 'reliable enough' to merit the conclusions drawn from them, 'reliable enough' for their purpose (Newton, 2009). If the purpose is to compare cohorts, then a standardised measure may be the most appropriate tool, but it is important to remember that such measures provide information about only a small sample of the curriculum.

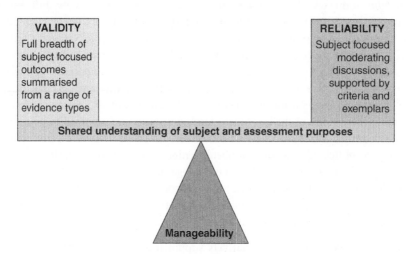

Figure 2.1   The Teacher Assessment Seesaw (adapted from Earle, 2017)

Figure 2.1 illustrates the following characteristics of teacher assessment.

- **Validity** focuses on content validity, providing a summary of the child's performance throughout the whole of the subject, to combat construct-under-representation. The suggestion here is that any summative reporting should be based on a range of evidence types, which aims to reduce the construct-irrelevance – e.g. whether the child can read the question (Black and Wiliam, 2012).

- **Reliability** is supported by reference to criteria, exemplars and moderating discussions where teachers consider from different perspectives what it means for a child to have met a particular objective. Such moderation meetings with colleagues support teachers to be confident and more consistent in their judgements, but it is important that these discussions are focused on the objectives to avoid unconscious bias from assumptions about the child's behaviour or performance in other subjects (Campbell, 2015).

- **Manageability** is explicitly highlighted at the base of the seesaw because if the 'weight' of number of assessments to satisfy both validity and reliability concerns are too onerous for the teacher, the system will collapse.

- **Shared understanding** is the 'beam' on which the other concepts rest, since assessment literacy, together with a secure grasp of progression in the subject area, underpin teacher assessment. To be able to balance concerns of validity and reliability, teachers require an understanding of what these terms mean for their context, what constitutes valid assessment and the criteria by which reliable judgements are made. Discussing formative and summative assessment, with reference to criteria and exemplar benchmarks, supports teachers to be confident and consistent in their judgements.

CONCLUSION

This chapter aimed to consider and define key terminology such as formative, summative, validity and reliability. Such terms are more than the 'names' of types of assessment; they form the principles by which assessment practice can be judged. The prevalence of such terms varies between contexts, as does their common usage. Thus, it is important to remember, as noted at the beginning of this chapter, that any discussion with colleagues should include a clarification of terminology to ensure a shared meaning.

The next two chapters take a closer look at formative assessment practices. Chapter 3 considers formative assessment from the perspective of the teacher, exploring practical strategies that can enhance teaching and learning. Chapter 4 will then look at assessment from the perspective of the pupils who are at the centre of all assessment processes.

REFERENCES

Assessment Reform Group (ARG) (1999) *Assessment for Learning: Beyond the Black Box*. Cambridge: University of Cambridge Faculty of Education.

Black, P and Harrison, C (2010) Formative assessment in science. In Osborne, J and Dillon, J (eds) *Good Practice in Science Teaching: What Research has to Say*. Maidenhead: Open University Press.

Black, P and Wiliam, D (1998) *Inside the Black Box*. London: GL Assessment.

Black, P and Wiliam, D (2012) The reliability of assessments. In Gardner, J (ed.) *Assessment and Learning* (2nd edn). London: SAGE.

Campbell, T (2015) Stereotyped at seven? Biases in teacher judgement of pupils' ability and attainment. *Journal of Social Policy*, *44*: 517–47.

Council for the Curriculum, Examinations and Assessment (CCEA) (2013) *Guidance on Assessment in the Primary School*. Belfast: CCEA.

Council for the Curriculum, Examinations and Assessment (CCEA) (2017) *Assessment Arrangements in Relation to Pupils in the Final Years of Key Stages 1 and 2 for Communication, Using Mathematics and Using ICT*. Belfast: CCEA.

Earle, S (2017) The challenge of balancing key principles in teacher assessment. *Journal of Emergent Science*, *12*: 41–7.

Filer, A and Pollard, A (2000) *The Social World of Pupil Assessment*. London: Continuum.

Gardner, J, Harlen, W, Hayward, L, Stobart, G with Montgomery, M (2010) *Developing Teacher Assessment*. Maidenhead: Open University Press.

Gipps, C (1994) *Beyond Testing: Towards a Theory of Educational Assessment*. London: Falmer Press.

Green, S and Oates, T (2009) Considering the alternatives to national assessment arrangements in England: possibilities and opportunities. *Educational Research*, *51*(2): 229–45.

Harlen, W (2007) *Assessment of Learning*. London: SAGE.

Harlen, W (2013) *Assessment and Inquiry-based Science Education: Issues in Policy and Practice*. Trieste: Global Network of Science Academies.

Hattie, J (2009) *Visible Learning: A Synthesis of Over 800 Meta-analyses Relating to Achievement*. Abingdon: Routledge.

Her Majesty's Stationery Office (HMSO) (2003) *Every Child Matters*. London: HMSO.

Isaacs, T, Zara, C and Herbert, G, with Coombs, S and Smith, C (2013) *Key Concepts in Educational Assessment*. London: SAGE.

Klenowski, V (2009) Assessment for learning revisited: an Asia-Pacific perspective. *Assessment in Education: Principles, Policy & Practice, 16*(3): 263–8.

Mansell, W, James, M and the Assessment Reform Group (2009) *Assessment in Schools: Fit for Purpose?* London: Teaching and Learning Research Programme.

McIntosh, J (2015) *Final Report of the Commission on Assessment without Levels*. London: DfE.

Messick, S. (1989) Meaning and values in test validation: the science and ethics of assessment. *American Educational Research Association, 18*(2): 5–11.

Newton, P (2009) The reliability of results from national curriculum testing in England. *Educational Research, 51*(2): 181–212.

Ofsted (2018a) *School Inspection Handbook*. London: Ofsted.

Ofsted (2018b) *Ofsted Inspection – Clarification for Schools*. London: Ofsted.

Oxford University Press (2018) *The Oxford English Dictionary: The Definitive Record of the English Language*. Available at: www.oed.com (accessed: 28/08/2018).

Pollard, A (2014) *Reflective Teaching in Schools* (4th edn). London: Bloomsbury.

Standards and Testing Agency (STA) (2015) *Government Response: Commission on Assessment without Levels*. London: STA.

Stobart, G (2008) *Testing Times: The Uses and Abuses of Assessment*. London: Routledge.

Stobart, G (2009) Determining validity in national curriculum assessments. *Educational Research, 51*(2): 161–79.

Stobart, G (2012) Validity in formative assessment. In Gardner, J (ed.) *Assessment and Learning* (2nd edn). London: SAGE.

Wiliam, D. (2003) National curriculum assessment: how to make it better. *Research Papers in Education, 18*(2): 129–36.

Wiliam, D (2018) *Embedded Formative Assessment* (2nd edn). Bloomington, IN: Solution Tree Press.

3

FORMATIVE USE OF ASSESSMENT BY TEACHERS

LYNN SALTER AND SARAH EARLE

---- PURPOSE OF THIS CHAPTER ----

In this chapter we will:

- examine how teachers use formative assessment to adapt their teaching and inform their planning;

- exemplify a range of approaches to formative assessment, including the use of elicitation strategies, questioning, giving feedback, learning intentions and success criteria.

INTRODUCTION

The key word in the title of this chapter is 'use'; it is essential that teachers make use of the information gathered through assessment. This 'use' might be within the lesson – for example, in the ongoing tweaking of questions or instructions; the tailoring and scaffolding of the learning experience; or the balancing of support and challenge for groups and individuals. This 'in the moment' use of assessment information is what makes great teaching, where feedback from the pupils is acted upon to shape the lesson: teaching is responsive. Formative assessment information can also be used after the lesson, to plan for next steps for teaching and learning experiences.

In their pioneering work on formative assessment, *Inside the Black Box*, Black and Wiliam (1998) firmly established the links between formative assessment and pupil progress. Subsequently, they worked with colleagues and teachers to identify questioning, feedback, learning intentions and success criteria, and peer and self-assessment as effective strategies for teachers to use to improve formative assessment (Black et al., 2002; Assessment Reform Group, 2002). Over 25 years later, this work continues to have relevance, as the teaching profession constantly seeks to deepen and improve their understanding of how to use these strategies to continuously improve children's learning.

This chapter will explore how teachers can make effective use of formative assessment before, during and after their lessons. A range of approaches and strategies for responsive teaching will be considered and exemplified.

WHY IS FORMATIVE ASSESSMENT IMPORTANT FOR TEACHERS?

Formative assessment or Assessment for Learning (AfL) has been a focus for research for some time. This research suggests that using and acting upon information gained from the children will have an impact on their learning (e.g. Black and Wiliam, 1998; Hattie and Clarke, 2019). As discussed in Chapter 2, formative assessment requires teachers to continually seek out and respond to information to enhance learning (Klenowski, 2009), with the teacher and the pupil considering progress and next steps. The role of the pupil will be explored in more detail in Chapter 4, with this chapter focusing on the role of the teacher.

As teachers, we want to create the most productive learning experiences for the children, and using formative assessment information can help us to do this. Formative assessment can help to inform the planning of lessons and the process of teaching. A helpful way to demonstrate this is by considering how teachers use formative assessment at each stage of the teaching process to maximise pupil learning outcomes, as set out in Table 3.1.

Table 3.1   Examples of ways to use formative assessment to inform planning and teaching

Before teaching	During teaching	After teaching
Gain clarity on what new learning is needed and set this out as a precise learning intention.	Build in time to respond to marking and reflect on how prior learning links to the new learning in the lesson.	Reflect critically on the progress made by the children: how well did they meet the learning intention and success criteria?
Calibrate the level of challenge needed for progress from varying pupil starting points.	Develop a shared understanding of the learning intention and success criteria.	Provide written feedback that enables children to make further individual progress.
Consider the scaffolds and support needed to enable all children to access the learning.	Ask questions to elicit understanding; explore misconceptions; adjust the level of challenge.	Identify children who need further support or additional challenge.
Connect the new learning to prior learning so that children use what they know to help them achieve the new learning objective.	Orchestrate and facilitate learning conversations with the children, providing specific feedback and guidance at every stage.	Provide time for children to respond to marking, within the next lesson or at other times in the school day.
Build new learning around the children's interests and meaningful contexts to engage and inspire them.	Intentionally target questions to particular children to move their learning forward.	Review the national curriculum requirements; identify gaps/areas for further learning progress.
Set out how learning will be assessed, being clear before teaching about what success in the lesson will look like.	Make micro-adjustments to planning and teaching based on the children's responses.	
Plan in advance the key questions that will be used to assess learning during the lesson.	Model what the children find difficult; work together and collaborate on finding solutions.	

Before teaching	During teaching	After teaching
Ensure that their own subject knowledge is secure and further developed where appropriate.	Scan and evaluate learning outcomes during the lesson and act on the findings. For example: • use mid-lesson plenaries to address misconceptions; • share examples of excellence and cascade this to other learners; • move children on to higher levels of challenge; • create 'fluid focus' groups to support common needs. Give children the chance to ask questions to clarify their learning and to explain what they are finding difficult. Collaboratively evaluate learning outcomes against the success criteria with the children.	Identify next steps in learning within the lesson sequence. Make macro-adjustments to planning to focus on the emerging needs.

Often children's progress is described as their learning journey, where the role of the teacher is to enable children to move their learning forward. Planning, teaching and assessment are seen as a cyclic process aimed at ensuring that children make progress towards the goals of the statutory curriculum or targets based on age-expected outcomes. Effective planning can start with teachers making a clear assessment of what the children know and can do, and comparing this to what they need to know to be able to do to demonstrate age-related expectations. This gap analysis helps teachers to become crystal clear about the increment of new learning being sought and this clarity, in turn, helps the teacher to create a logical sequence of lessons that step the children from where they are to where they need to be. As the diagram below illustrates (Figure 3.1), your key objective when teaching the sequence or unit is to ensure that children make progress from their prior learning position towards the desired outcome, by enabling them to develop the skills and concepts they need to close this gap.

By defining the desired learning outcomes, as a teacher you know exactly where you would like the learning to go, allowing you to respond to the children's needs as they emerge. You can 'let go' of the learning more because you will be able to judge when children's questions and suggestions for approaches to their learning align to the required outcome. Learning can become a more collaborative process as you work with your learners to achieve commonly agreed success criteria. Progress in lessons become more visible to both you and the children because the 'destination' of the learning is clear. Hattie (2012) argues that the most important use that teachers can make of formative assessment is to know the impact of their teaching on learning; to make 'learning visible' for both themselves and for their learners. When you as the teacher know where the learning is going, then you are able to use information gathered from formative assessment to confidently

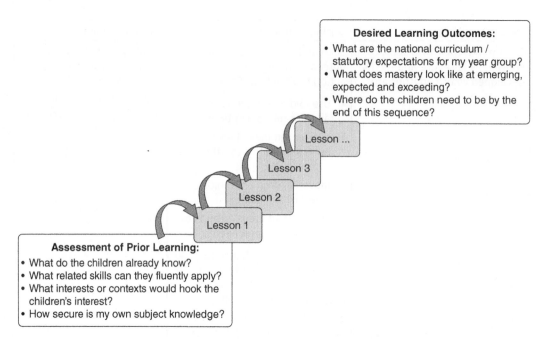

Desired Learning Outcomes:
- What are the national curriculum / statutory expectations for my year group?
- What does mastery look like at emerging, expected and exceeding?
- Where do the children need to be by the end of this sequence?

Lesson ...

Lesson 3

Lesson 2

Lesson 1

Assessment of Prior Learning:
- What do the children already know?
- What related skills can they fluently apply?
- What interests or contexts would hook the children's interest?
- How secure is my own subject knowledge?

Figure 3.1   Using formative assessment to plan for progression

make micro-adjustments to your planning as you teach and to evaluate outcomes after lessons to make macro-adjustments between teaching episodes.

Having established the importance of placing formative assessment at the heart of planning for pupil progress, the following sections consider how to use a range of formative assessment strategies to enable you to move learning forward. The section begins by examining the important role that elicitation plays as a formative assessment process, followed by exploration of questioning, feedback, learning intentions and success criteria. The remaining key formative assessment strategy of peer and self-assessment is explored in Chapter 4.

STRATEGIES FOR FORMATIVE ASSESSMENT

ELICITATION

Children come into your class with a range of prior experience and understanding. They may have in-depth knowledge of a topic from previous class work or a home interest, or have never heard the terms you are using before. They may also have developed their own personal explanations, which do not match the accepted view: misconceptions or alternative conceptions – for example, that going north means going up hill or that the sun turns into the moon at night. To teach effectively, it is important to be aware of such ideas and ascertain the starting points for the pupils in your class. There is a range of techniques for eliciting children's understanding; some common ones are listed in Table 3.2, with further discussion about teacher questioning below. The techniques listed in the table are divided into open and closed strategies, which can be useful at different times.

Table 3.2 *Common elicitation and assessment strategies*

More open elicitation strategies (What do they know?)	More closed assessment strategies (Do they know x?)
Dialogue Observation of pupils KWL grid (Know, Would like to know, Learnt) Mind map/thought shower Pupil drawing or model making Pupil question raising Open investigations Pupil presentation	Written or oral question and answer activities: tests, online multiple-choice quiz, quick-fire teacher questions, whole-class electronic voting - e.g. Plickers Cloze-the-gap activities Matching or grouping activities Diagrams with pre-made labels Challenge tasks Tasks with pre-defined success criteria

Open elicitation strategies are useful if the aim is to find out *what pupils know* – for example, at the start of a topic to inform planning, or at the end of topic to summarise learning. More closed assessment strategies are useful if the aim is to find out *whether pupils know* a particular thing, like times tables or names of continents. Torrance and Prior (1998) call these intentions 'divergent' and 'convergent', whereby divergent activities spread out to explore a range of pupil ideas and convergent activities close in on the checking of particular concepts. The Teacher Assessment in Primary Science (TAPS) project adds a third category of 'focused assessment' (Earle et al. 2018), which includes a clear focus for the activity, but also allows for a diversity of outcomes, making it a fruitful way to find out about children's attainment for a particular curriculum outcome.

QUESTIONING AND DIALOGUE

In teaching, we ask a range of different questions to support learning in a variety of ways. This can be to open up learning conversations; to elicit understanding; to give learners the opportunity to practise and demonstrate their skills and understanding; and to challenge their thinking and deepen learning. Rowe (1974) reminds us of the importance of ensuring that we leave appropriate 'wait time', to give children appropriate time to consider the question and formulate their responses. Others (e.g. Clarke, 2014) would go further and advocate the importance of giving children time to orally rehearse and socially construct their responses together as an essential element to the learning occurring. In the previous section on elicitation, the importance of questioning to elicit prior learning has been explored. This begs the question: what is the difference between posing questions to stimulate discussions and posing questions for formative assessment? The distinction centres on how the teacher uses the information; the purpose and intent of assessment for learning questions are to find out about children's understandings and proficiency in using skills and concepts. When teachers act on the answers to improve their understanding, provide additional, specific modelling or problems aimed at addressing misconceptions or taking learning forward, then they have asked a high-quality assessment for learning question.

It is good practice to plan these questions in advance, considering when and how in the lesson you will use them to check pupil understanding. It is also useful to have discussed with a colleague or thought about how to provide further support or additional challenge. Elicitation questions are often asked at the start of the lesson to activate prior learning and connect it to new learning. For example, a teacher whose lesson required children to exchange and regroup when calculating is likely to ask questions at the start of the lesson to check rapid recall of facts, as well as probing their understanding of place value. This questioning both signposts the need for the children to use these related skills to support their new learning, and acts as an elicitation of pupil understanding for the teacher, who can then tailor the follow-up activities to meet the children's specific needs. Questions about the unit, previous day's learning or learning completed earlier in the year are also often included to both reinforce and assess retention of prior learning.

Questions during the lesson may be used to identify and address misconceptions as they arise, or to move learning on by asking a more challenging question. At the end of a lesson, good AfL questioning approaches help both the teacher and the children to consider how successful they have been in achieving the new learning. As well as considering what questions you will plan and ask as a teacher, it is also important to consider what opportunities you can provide for the children to craft and ask questions for themselves and each other. Wiliam and Leahy (2015) emphasise the importance of giving children these opportunities, highlighting research that shows that giving children time to devise questions about what they have been learning and finding answers to them is a much more effective way to raise achievement than asking them to spend time answering questions in practice tests.

The table below sets out a number of formative questioning strategies for you to consider when planning your lessons. This list is not intended to be exhaustive, but rather to prompt your thinking on the variety of ways you can use formative assessment questions to have a strong impact on pupil progress as you teach.

Table 3.3   Formative assessment questions and actions

Formative assessment questioning strategies	Teacher actions to enhance learning
Ask hinge questions Which of these questions can you answer? – show me on your whiteboards. Which of these questions can you do? Which is the most difficult question for you and why? Which is the right answer from a list of multiple-choice answers.	• Start the learning from what the children already know and can do. • Decide appropriate challenge level for independent skills practice. • Set up a fluid focus group to address common needs. • Spot children's misconceptions early in in lesson.
Ask open questions with several right answers How many ways do you know how to . . . ? Show me on your whiteboards.	• Moves away from the idea that there is only one right answer. • Challenges children to widen their thinking and show a wider range of their understanding.
Pose spot the mistake(s) questions: Compare these two answers. Which is right and which is wrong? How do you know?	• Engages children in recognising common errors and correcting them. • Encourages a culture of learning from mistakes.

Formative assessment questioning strategies	Teacher actions to enhance learning
Ask thinking questions: What do you think . . . ? How do you think . . . ? Why do you think . . . ? Do you agree or disagree? Why?	• Opens the discussion to a variety of answers. • Avoids the worry/threat of being wrong; it is not about what you know but what you think. • Allows teachers to have a window into the way children think.
Ask delving questions: Explain your reasoning. Tell me more about how you solved it. Why is your answer a good one?	• Deepens teacher understanding of what and why children are finding concepts and skills difficult to master. • Offers an immediate opportunity to correct misconceptions and deepen learning.
Provide children with the opportunity to pose questions: Write questions that you would like to find out the answers to in our unit on xx? Write a question that you can do now that you couldn't at the start of the lesson. Write a question that you would like to be able to do by the end of the next lesson.	• Collect these in and use the questions to inform planning and to shape follow-up lessons. • Gives children ownership for their learning. • Provides the opportunity to target learning to both the curiosities and specific needs of the children.
Pupil conferencing Setting out specific questions to explore with a child/target group of children. Encourage the child to talk about their thinking processes, use of equipment and methods they are using to solve the problem. Find out about their learning dispositions: do they like or dislike this subject?	• Focus is on how the learners arrive at answers, not on the right answers themselves. • Supports teachers in diagnosing and addressing specific misconceptions. • Provides useful information on pupils' mind sets and confidence levels. • Outcomes inform future planning and interventions.

Case study 3.1 below provides an example of the conferencing process in action and the impact its use had on planning, teaching and learning.

— CASE STUDY 3.1 MATHS CONFERENCING —

While on her PGCE at Bath Spa University, Lauren Singleton used maths conferencing as a way of having a structured learning conversation with profile children to assess their prior knowledge. During the conferencing sessions, Lauren posed a number of maths questions related to key year group expectations for number and calculation. She provided the children with maths resources for them to use to support their problem solving and asked the children to talk her through their

(Continued)

(Continued)

thinking as they worked through the steps of the problem. By using this process, Lauren was able to find out to what extent each child had a deep, mastery level understanding of the mathematics and to what extent their understanding was what Skemp (1978) terms as 'instrumental understanding', where they were following 'rules without reasons'. Questioning and observing children as they worked enabled her to precisely identify their misconceptions and gave her real clarity about what she needed to teach to help the children make progress. The process also enabled her to find out about the children's attitude and confidence levels towards their maths learning.

For example, with a group of Year 1 profile children, Lauren was surprised to find that none of her three children - who were representative of high, middle and low prior attainers - could distinguish between odd and even numbers. This challenged her to consider why this concept was so difficult for the children and to consider new ways to present the concept to the children; she then created a specific intervention that enabled the children to overcome this barrier. She found that using conferencing in this way had the benefit of helping her consider more deeply her choice of pedagogical approach so that her teaching closely matched the children's needs.

In another instance when working with Year 4 profile children, Lauren found that the children had developed a definite preference for solving calculations and that they were reluctant to use other methods even when they found the problem posed very difficult. For example, when working with one Year 4 girl, she found that although she could apply her understanding of number bonds to complete problems involving tu + tu – for example, to successfully add 36 + 64 together - she was not successful adding larger numbers that required her to bridge through 10, 100 and 1,000. This enabled her to pinpoint both the misconception and her lack of fluency in moving between methods (see Table 3.4). She also found that she needed to overcome the child's reluctance to use equipment and visual models that were further barriers to her learning. Lauren used this assessment to inform her planning for the sequence of lessons for the whole class in which she included opportunities for all children to use equipment to help them to develop a strong, relational understanding of the exchange and regrouping process.

Table 3.4   *Excerpt from the maths conferencing: pupil responses and teacher comments*

Addition	
Questions jotted on mini-whiteboard: 64 + 36 640 + 36 64 + 79 + 36 378 + 562 999 + 999 **Teacher instructions:** Use either a mental or written method to solve these problems. Talk me through your thinking and the steps you are following as that is more important to me than the answers. You can solve them in any order and with any method you choose.	 *Figure 3.2 Bella's working out*

> **Notes/comments**
>
> Bella chose to do the question 999 + 999 first. She answered this question orally as 1,800. Bella was reminded that the number 999 was close to 1,000. With this prompt she wrote 1,000 + 1,000 = 2,000. Of all the problems she attempted to answer, she found this one particularly difficult. In observing and listening in to her approach, it became clear that Bella had a secure understanding of place value and partitioning to help her add. But she was not confident with the process of exchanging and regrouping, particularly when more than one exchange was needed in larger numbers. She also lacked the number sense to alter her preferred strategy to use rounding and compensating to solve this problem mentally.

Calculation questions source: Askew et al., 2015, p14.

From her experience, Lauren concluded that maths conferencing was a very effective AfL process that enabled her to discover the children's capabilities; gave her an in-depth understanding of their specific misconceptions; helped her consider appropriate teaching approaches; and provided her with an awareness of the children's confidence and attitude towards maths learning. She found that asking questions to give her insights into the children's understanding of maths processes and concepts was much more useful than focusing on whether the children got the right answer. She was also able to use the findings from her three profile children as a microcosm for the knowledge and understandings of the whole class. Hence, maths conferencing supported her not only in planning specific interventions for the individual children, but also in sculpting her overall planning for the whole class. She has continued to use maths conferencing in her NQT year first to build children's fluency in new concepts and then to provide them with high-quality problem solving and reasoning contexts so they develop deep mastery.

LEARNING INTENTIONS AND SUCCESS CRITERIA

Wiliam (2018) suggests that in writing learning intentions, teachers are setting out *what will be learned* and that adding success *criteria* sets out *how the learning* will be achieved. Clarke (2014) and Hattie (2012) highlight the importance of being clear and concise in defining the new learning you wish to see and in showing children from the outset what success looks like. Armed with clear learning intentions and success criteria, you know the exact 'destination' or outcome you are aiming for the children to reach. This clarity enables you to ensure that your teacher subject knowledge is deep and accurate; it helps you make clear choices for what and how you will model new concepts to move the children on in their learning; and it enables you to make micro-adjustments as you teach to address misconceptions as they arise or enhance the level of challenge needed to meet the children's needs. Clear, shared success criteria also provide a benchmark for both you and the children to judge how well the learning has been demonstrated, as will be also be noted in Chapter 4 when considering peer and self-assessment.

Creating clear learning intentions and related success criteria is easier said than done; there is an art to ensuring they lead to great learning outcomes for the children. From her research and work with teachers, Clarke (2014) advises that learning intentions should be context-free and focus on the new skill or concept to enable children to connect their learning to a variety of contexts. Clarke goes on to argue that setting a 'context-free' learning intention fundamentally changes the way that success criteria are written because they become tightly related to the new skill or concept rather than linked to a particular context. To illustrate these points, consider the way that the learning intentions change the focus of the success criteria in Table 3.5. When evaluating achievement and progress against the context-specific example, the conversations and feedback are intrinsically linked to 'Horrid Henry' with the question at the centre of the assessment being 'How well has the child described Horrid Henry?' In the second example, the focus for assessment for learning is 'How well does the child understand the process of writing a character description?'

Table 3.5   The difference between context-specific and context-free objectives

Context-specific	Skills/concept-specific
Learning intention: Can I write a character description for Horrid Henry? Success criteria:	Learning intention: Can I write a character description? Success criteria:
• Look closely at a picture of Horrid Henry. • Make a list of adjectives and phrases to describe Henry's appearance and personality. • Use your list to write a quality paragraph about Horrid Henry.	• Look carefully at a picture of the character. • Make a list of words and phrases to describe the character's appearance and personality. • Use your lists to write a quality paragraph, describing the character.

Writing success criteria also needs considerable thought and careful crafting. In the example in Table 3.5, the success criteria are written as a set of *'process or procedural' criteria*. They set up a recipe for success, giving the learners clear steps to follow and to check their learning against. Alternatively, success criteria can also be set out as *'product or outcome' criteria*, with the statements providing guidance on expectations of the quantity and quality of the learning. For example, you could set the success criteria as a set of must, should, could statements, or hot, spicy and super spicy challenge statements. Writing success criteria in this way can support differentiation of the learning and gives the children clear guidance on where their learning meets or exceeds expectations. It gives you the opportunity to vary the context and type of challenge the learners meet as they progress during the lesson. Many proponents of outcome criteria highlight the benefits of giving the children *choice* in the level of challenge and the opportunity to move through challenges levels within lessons so that learning is not 'capped' for those with low prior attainment in other areas.

As you write learning intentions and success criteria, there are a number of other considerations to take into account to ensure that they have the desired impact on learning outcomes and enable you to assess these outcomes. For example, you will need to consider whether your word choice and language are accessible to the children. You will also need to decide on how many success criteria to include and work to keep these focused on the 'new outcomes' you wish to see. Adjusting the criteria to focus on the misconceptions you notice as you teach a sequence will help to ensure that your success criteria are tailored specifically to the needs of your children. This will more powerfully move learning forward rather than applying a 'generic' set from a published scheme of work.

It is worth noticing how writing the learning intention as a question supports formative assessment by inviting both you and the children to answer the question, 'How well has this outcome been achieved?' The success criteria can then act as a checklist for you to use to make these judgements and to help you give specific guidance on how each child could improve further. Building time during lessons to give feedback and further guidance on how to achieve the success criteria have more impact on outcomes than waiting until the end of the lesson. For example, a well-placed mid-lesson plenary where you explore a child's work under the visualiser can cascade this success across the class; or taking time for a 'pit stop' to model a specific part of a maths problem you have noticed most children are finding difficult will help the children learn from their mistakes before the end of the lesson. Using success criteria to evaluate the learning will not only help you to give clear guidance, but also offers you a framework to use to train the children to reflect on the quality of their learning, as will be discussed in Chapter 4 when considering the benefits of engaging children in peer and self-assessment.

Key points from this section are summarised in Table 3.6, which provides a quick reference checklist as a useful starting point. Of course, the context of the lesson should be taken into account when applying this guidance, since not all points will be appropriate for every lesson. For example, revealing the aim of learning that metals conduct electricity removes the practical purpose of testing materials in science. Similarly, a pre-designated model of excellence may not be appropriate for creative outputs (see Case study 6.1).

Table 3.6   Quick reference checklist for creating effective learning intentions and success criteria

Checklist to support development of effective learning intentions and success criteria
Points to consider when creating learning intentions and success criteria.
• Is your learning intention a *clear* statement of the *new learning*?
• Is it written in *child-friendly language*?
• Is the learning intention *context-free*?
• Have you written the *learning intention as a question*?
• Have you set out *process success criteria*: the *steps for success* to guide the children's learning?
• Have you shown what *excellence looks like* at the start of the lesson (if appropriate)?
• Have you kept the *number* of success criteria *manageable and achievable* for your learners?
• Are you and the children *evaluating progress* against the lesson's *specific success criteria*?

EFFECTIVE FEEDBACK

Feedback is the process by which the learner receives information back from the teacher regarding their learning. This could be oral or written, group or individual, at the time or later. It could include comments, instructions, grades or examples to work from. Whatever the means of feedback, it is only effective if the pupils are able to act on it – for example, to improve their writing or add shading to their observational drawing. Coaching is a good way to think about feedback, with the coach looking closely at what the learner is doing and providing guidance about what to do next. This could be simply providing a 'way in' to the task for those who are not sure about where to start, or lead to a more extensive unpicking of the task outcome. The guidance provides focused next steps that the learner can understand to be able to hone their skill or move forward in their thinking.

Written feedback in the form of marking has received much attention in recent years. When research showed that comments were more likely than grades to supported learning (e.g. Butler, 1988), extended comment marking became the vogue. Such marking not only had implications for teacher workload, it also required class time for the marking to be acted upon, which could only happen if the feedback was specific and manageable. Providing such feedback is difficult because it not only relies on a secure understanding of progression steps in the subject, it also requires an understanding of the needs of the individual pupil. Impactful comment marking takes time and thus cannot be an expectation for every lesson: *feedback should be more work for the recipient than the donor* (Wiliam, 2018, p144). One school's development of marking and feedback can be found in Case study 3.2.

CASE STUDY 3.2 REPLACING MARKING WITH FEEDBACK

Andy Moor, Principal at St Bernard's RC Primary School in Cheshire, has worked with his staff to develop practices that are more focused on feedback rather than on marking. The staff took part in a school-based research project to explore alternative approaches to marking, after they found that the marking burden had become too cumbersome, with teachers working late into the night to 'feed the policy' rather than focus on pupil learning (Moor, 2017).

They began by selecting one group each lesson to receive oral feedback rather than feedback in books. While this was well received, it did not stop staff from feeling they had to spend hours intensively marking books, as they had done for many years, so Andy took the radical step of asking his staff to completely stop marking, to break the habit and replace it with a range of other techniques, such as:

- sharing examples of work with a visualiser to discuss and refine before turning to their own, supporting peer and self-assessment;
- use of questioning – for example, asking 'hingepoint' or multiple-choice questions, to which pupils respond using ABCD cards or use of Plickers;
- rather than 'respond to marking' time, there is group verbal feedback time;
- pupils or groups with a 'gap' are identified during the lesson or when books are put into piles at the end.

In the children's books, you do not see teacher comments, but you do see evidence of children editing their work. Changing the day-to-day routine and expectations regarding marking has been a whole-school endeavour, which has moved the focus from evidencing the teacher feedback to evidencing the learning and embedding formative assessment.

Feedback is not synonymous with marking and there are many other strategies for providing feedback to pupils – for example:

- whole-class mini-plenaries or pauses during the lesson to revisit the success criteria and discuss difficulties;

- individual or group discussions during the lesson to explore successes and next steps;

- use of self- and peer assessment against success criteria;

- exploration of an example of an outcome to identify key points;

- individual or group discussions in the following lesson;

- choice of follow-up tasks that provide practice on elements.

Whether feedback is written, verbal or involves provision of revised tasks, it should be focused on the development of learning. Since it is essential to provide time for the learner to act on feedback, there is an argument for trying to find ways for this to happen within the lesson.

CONCLUSION

The key messages in this chapter chime with Wiliam (2018) who maintains that teacher's use of formative assessment builds the bridge between teaching and learning. For formative assessment to have an impact, teachers need to use and act upon what they learn by applying the different strategies at every stage of the teaching process, in order to enable and empower children to improve and enhance their skills, knowledge and understanding. Assessment for learning strategies need to be used by teachers dynamically as they teach to flexibly respond to children's needs as they arise. Using AfL to plan for progression, with the final destination clear from the outset of the teaching sequence, gives teachers the confidence to come away from the detail of plans, to follow children's curiosities, interests and questions. Knowing the final destination of the learning provides the teacher with the freedom to orchestrate and guide children to the outcome, allowing them to travel there on their own paths.

The overriding aim of teachers' use of formative assessment is to put learning and children at the heart of teaching. By sharing what success looks like and matching this clearly with the children's interest and needs, both you and the children can collaboratively, creatively and flexibly work together to achieve the learning goals. The next chapter focuses on how to develop and engage your children in formative assessment so that they feel more ownership and empowerment for their learning.

REFERENCES

Askew, M, Bishop, S, Christie, C, Eaton, S, Griffin, P and Morgan, D (2015) Teaching for mastery: questions, tasks and activities to support assessment, Year 4. Crown copyright: text. Oxford University Press: copyright design and illustration. Available online at: www.ncetm.org.uk/public/files/23305622/Mastery_Assessment_Y4_Low_Res.pdf (last accessed: 28/1/19).

Assessment Reform Group (ARG) (2002) *Assessment for Learning: 10 Principles: Research-based Principles to Guide Classroom Practice*. Cambridge: University of Cambridge School of Education.

Black, P and Wiliam, D (1998) *Inside the Black Box: Raising Standards Through Classroom Assessment*. London: King's College School of Education.

Black, P, Harrison, C, Lee, C, Marshall, B and Wiliam, D (2002) *Working Inside the Black Box*. London: GL Assessment.

Butler, R (1988) Enhancing and undermining intrinsic motivation: the effects of task-involving and ego-involving evaluation on interest and performance. *British Journal of Educational Psychology, 58*: 1–14.

Clarke, S (2014) *Outstanding Formative Assessment: Culture and Practice*. London: Hodder Education.

Earle, S, Qureshi, A, Rodger, P and Sampey, S (2018) Supporting assessment across school. In Serret, N and Earle, S (eds) *ASE Guide to Primary Science Education* (4th edn). Hatfield: Association for Science Education.

Hattie, J (2012) *Visible Learning for Teachers: Maximising Impact on Achievement*. Abingdon: Routledge.

Hattie, J and Clarke, S (2019) *Visible Learning Feedback*. Abingdon: Routledge.

Klenowski, V (2009) Assessment for Learning revisited: an Asia-Pacific perspective. *Assessment in Education: Principles, Policy & Practice, 16*(3): 263–8.

Moor, A (2017) Balancing workload, assessment and feedback in the primary classroom. *Impact, 1*: 30–3.

Rowe, MB (1974) Wait time and rewards as instructional variables, their influence on language, logic and fate control. *Journal of Research in Science Teaching, 1*: 81–94.

Skemp, R (1978) Relational understanding and instrumental understanding. *The Arithmetic Teacher, 26*(3): 9–15.

Torrance, H and Prior, J (1998) *Investigating Formative Assessment*. Maidenhead: Open University Press.

Wiliam, D (2018) *Embedded Formative Assessment* (2nd edn). Bloomington, IN: Solution Tree Press.

Wiliam, D and Leahy, S (2015) *Embedding Formative Assessment: Practical Techniques for K–12 Classrooms*. West Palm Beach, FL: Learning Sciences International.

4
FORMATIVE USE OF ASSESSMENT BY PUPILS

NIAMH MCGROGAN AND SARAH EARLE

┌───┐
PURPOSE OF THIS CHAPTER

In this chapter we will:

- develop an understanding of peer and self-assessment as interactive formative assessment processes;

- consider children's perceptions of formative assessment;

- explore effective implementation of peer and self-assessment.
└───┘

INTRODUCTION

In this chapter, we will explore assessment from the perspective of the children, considering the ways in which they can use formative assessment to develop and take ownership of their learning. We will begin by reflecting on the way in which formative assessment can be interactive, through the use of peer and self-assessment. Consideration of children's views and understanding of the formative assessment process help to inform the effective design and implementation of peer and self-assessment in the classroom. Pupil understanding of learning objectives and expected outcomes, which were discussed in the previous chapter, are a key precursor to effective peer and self-assessment. This chapter will take this understanding forward, to focus on strategies that recognise the children as active participants and *owners of their own learning* (Wiliam, 2018).

PEER AND SELF-ASSESSMENT AS AN INTERACTIVE PROCESS

There is a range of strategies that teachers can employ to help build a picture of the children's understanding, to inform planning and future learning activities. The process of formative assessment is complex, and consideration of these complexities can ensure that strategies are not done *to* the children, but *with* them, and learning is subsequently co-constructed. As Boaler (2000, p381) notes, children's active participation in formative assessment processes are key as they can *negotiate, shape and reflect* as learners: *the emphasis in AfL is very much on involving pupils in their learning* (Crichton and McDaid, 2016, p191). However, collaborative learning is more than bringing groups of children together. It requires engagement on the part of the children in purposeful and focused activities, facilitated by consideration of the interpersonal aspects of the assessment process on the part of the teacher.

Peer assessment and self-assessment are two formative assessment strategies that will be the focus of this chapter and that demonstrate the interactive nature of the process. They are often considered together as they explicitly and directly involve the children in assessment. The former involves children working collaboratively with their peers to assess each other's learning, suggesting strengths as well as areas to develop in their work and support the construction of knowledge in a social context. Self-assessment is the child's own continual assessment of their learning, identifying what they have achieved and how they can move their learning further forward. These assessment strategies can empower children to view learning as a process over which they can exert some control and, used effectively, can enhance teacher assessment and promote scholarship.

The importance of children's participation in formative assessment is an intrinsic aspect of the process, as it is *clearly more than a set of procedures* (Miller and Lavin, 2007, p4). Any formative approach used to assess learning requires the children's participation in some way, often through responding to adults, but peer and self-assessments allow children to assume a lead role in the process. In addition, engaging in the process can support children developing autonomy and independence, promote self-regulation and increase a sense of ownership in their learning. Metacognition – thinking about one's own thinking – requires the child to step back and consider how they are learning, rather than just what they are learning. Opportunities to help pupils to develop their metacognitive skills include explicit discussion of thought processes with children, providing time for evaluation and reflection, together with modelling of metacognition yourself (e.g. 'Where shall I start?' 'What do I already know that could help me?' 'I'm struggling with this part, what shall I do to help myself?') (EEF, 2018). It is also significant to note that this is *not confined to older pupils . . . [successful] strategies [can] involve children from the age of 5 upward in assessing their work* (Harlen and Qualter, 2018, p242); the children's active participation is key regardless of the age group. This can be encouraged through *the mutual construction of achievement and improvement* (Cowie, 2005, p15) and an important consideration is the interplay between various elements of the process. Cowie determined that, from children's perspectives, the purpose of assessment also encompasses the desire to please the teacher, fear of failure, comparing themselves to others and issues around (mis)trusting peers. These important factors are considered throughout the chapter when exploring how to implement peer and self-assessment in the classroom.

DESIGNING PEER AND SELF-ASSESSMENT ACTIVITIES

Peer or self-assessment strategies in the classroom must be purposeful in terms of the children's learning and how the outcomes will serve to inform teacher assessment. Therefore, the design of an assessment activity begins at the *planning* stage, built into the lesson to enhance the learning taking place. Therefore, questions such as 'What is this activity for?', 'How will this activity enhance the learning?' and 'What will the outcomes inform?' should form part of the planning process (see Table 4.1).

Deciding to use a peer or self-assessment approach to formative assessment in a lesson is only the first step. Consideration should then be given to the assessment activity itself; there is a range of techniques and strategies that encompass these approaches and the most appropriate activity is context dependent. Using the same assessment activity repeatedly in lessons could render the activity ineffective if pupil motivation is lost through repetition. It is therefore important to remember that one size does not necessarily fit all, and the assessment activity should be tailored to the learning and the children. *To say that an assessment is a good assessment or that a task is a good task is like saying that a medical test is a good test; each can provide useful information only under certain circumstances* (Pellegrino et al., 2001, p222).

Table 4.1   Questions for planning peer/self-assessment

Reason
• How does this activity support learning?
• How does it link to the lesson focus?
• What are the limitations of this assessment activity?
• What insight will it give to children's learning/understanding?
Design
• What is this activity assessing?
• What will the activity look like in the classroom?
• What criteria will the children use to assess?
• How will the assessment be recorded?
• How will the children be supported to understand the reasons for the assessment?
Implement
• What resources are needed?
• How will the class dynamic be managed?
• What will good quality feedback look like?
• How will the outcomes of the assessment be used (to inform planning/teacher assessment of progress)?

Clarity at this point will facilitate the children's understanding of the purpose of the assessment and support their engagement with it. Supporting the understanding of why and how the peer or self-assessment process works can be achieved through effective *modelling* over time. *Students need to be explicitly scaffolded* (Smith and Hackling, 2016, p151), so using, for example, an anonymised piece of work from a previous year, teachers can display the work and model the process of assessment against specific criteria, verbalising their thinking at each step to support the children's understanding. Included in this process can be an examination of the quality of the feedback being given, identifying that which best supports learning. This can develop into marking as a whole class and exploring the process before children then move to peer or self-assessment without adult support. Embedding a clear understanding of how to peer assess effectively takes time. Modelling may need to happen a number of times before the children trust the value and quality of their own and each other's feedback, and the building of this trust is an essential component of formative assessment (Foley, 2013).

Many children find the process of formative assessment productive and purposeful, allowing them to view their learning through the eyes of the peers and in doing so, learn from their mistakes (Bozkurt and Demir, 2013). However, trust and respect are important considerations that impact on children's willingness to interact with teachers and/or peers throughout the formative assessment process (Rudduck et al., 1996); essentially, children need to be able to trust that teachers and peers will respond to their contributions with respect. Social pressures and group dynamics play significant roles and children need to feel secure in their *belief that the environment is safe for interpersonal risks, that is, group members feel safe enough to say, do, and ask what they think is good (psychological safety), and a feeling of mutual dependence according to the task (interdependence)* (Foley, 2013).

To support the transition to assessing without adult support, it can be helpful to offer *prompts* that the children can use to write their feedback. Such prompts could be 'I notice that . . . ' 'There were some . . . ' or 'This could be improved by using . . .'. In the case of peer assessment, prompts not only support the child assessing to give constructive feedback, but also support the child receiving the feedback to recognise that it is purposeful and structured to support learning. Keeping the prompts focused on the work rather than the child – i.e. 'There were some . . . ' rather than 'You used some . . . ' can begin to mitigate some of the issues of (mis)trust and fear of failure, as the feedback is focused on the learning rather than on the child. These prompts can provide a bridge between the modelled peer assessment and the children peer assessing without support. Again, this takes time and the use of prompts may be necessary for some time before the concept of giving and receiving constructive feedback focused on learning is fully embedded.

An important consideration is that the interactive element to formative assessment goes beyond just involving the children; children consider assessment to have *cognitive, affective and social purposes and consequences* (Cowie, 2005, p146), so it can be valuable to examine how the *grouping* of children potentially affects the process. The dynamics within a classroom play a part in the interactions (Foley, 2013) and children need to feel comfortable sharing their work with their peer. For example, in an English lesson, children can be paired together to read and assess the other's writing. Careful, deliberate pairing is important in peer assessment as children need to trust that the other will recognise their efforts, that they will provide constructive feedback and that identified areas to develop are opportunities for learning rather than an indication of failure. Children can be paired or encouraged to choose their own partner; in either case, it is essential that children are clear on the purpose of the peer assessment and the criteria being used. It is important to take time to explain to children *why* peer assessment is being used for the activity and *how* it can support learning and move it forward. Clarity of the intent of the assessment can give it purpose and meaning for the children and facilitate them placing a higher value on the activity.

Equally important is the *criteria* the children will use to assess the writing. In much the same way as lessons should be pitched appropriately for the class, so too must the assessment process. Multiple criteria, which includes all the aspects of the writing a teacher would assess, can prove daunting; peer assessment does not have to be as detailed or in depth as teacher assessment. Instead, 'precise and concise' can be an effective mantra. Children should assess the work with a precise focus on one or two aspects of the writing, such as the use of adverbs and accurate syntax, with reassurance that other criteria are equally important but will be teacher assessed.

This allows the children to trust that the activity, and consequently their partner, is focused on learning. The peer feedback being given the same regard as teacher feedback can also foster ownership and engagement in the activity. This precision also allows the assessment activity to be concise and achievable within a set time frame and the contributions of everyone to the assessment process are clear and valued.

The use of clear criteria also supports the *consolidation* of learning. If children are to assess adverbs in another's work, for example, they need to be clear themselves on what an adverb is, how to use adverbs correctly and what their purpose is. Therefore, both children in the pair are continually consolidating their own knowledge and understanding through supporting the learning of the other. This is an example of the overlap that can occur between peer and self-assessment; they do not always need to occur as separate processes. Children can find self-assessment challenging because it is hard to spot errors in their own work. By assessing others' work, children can then use this experience to turn a critical eye to their own learning and assess it in a similar way. By either beginning with a peer assessment activity and then moving to self-assessment immediately after, or working with a partner to assess their own and their peer's work collaboratively, children can begin to review with a greater sense of objectivity, finding the same strengths and areas to develop in their own work in the same way as they do their partner's.

Examples of peer and self-assessment strategies are listed in Table 4.2, with practices in two schools explored in more depth in Case studies 4.1 and 4.2.

Table 4.2 Examples of strategies for self- and peer assessment

Self-assessment strategies	Peer feedback strategies
Hand signals or **'Thumbs up, thumbs down'** In this activity, the children give an overall assessment of their understanding by using hand signals such as holding their thumbs up or down. If they are unsure or feel their understanding is incomplete, they hold their thumbs in between up and down. Such 'public' announcements require careful managing of the classroom climate, as will be discussed further below.	**'Two stars and a wish'** or a **'Feedback sandwich'** Peers identify two strengths and one aspect to develop. Such feedback may be provided orally or on a sticky note, not needing to be permanently recorded. To support the development of peer assessment, some sticky note examples can be shared to identify features of supportive feedback. *Also see below.*
'Traffic lights' for self-review Colour coding of confidence levels can involve placing books or name cards/pegs on coloured paper or in coloured trays, or colouring in a box on the work itself. The teacher may use this information to help structure groups for feedback or subsequent activities. *Also see Case study 4.1.*	**Peer checking** Before handing in work, a peer uses a checklist to double-check that all the required elements are in place. This helps both parties to pay closer attention to the learning outcomes.

(Continued)

Table 4.2 (Continued)

Self-assessment strategies	Peer feedback strategies
'Traffic lights' as signals in the lesson Traffic light self-assessment can also be utilised within the lesson to provide a signal to the teacher to slow down or pause to explain further. Pupils can have coloured cards, cups or blocks which they display on the table to provide feedback to the teacher regarding their understanding of the lesson. A pupil displaying green may be asked to help explain the concept to the class.	**'Plenary buddies' or 'Think, pair, share'** Plenaries can take place in the middle or the end of a lesson. Throughout the lesson, the children consider an aspect of the learning or a set question, explore this with a partner and then share their understanding. At the end of the lesson, they can summarise the learning in the lesson to their partner.
'Four corners' This activity involves first labelling the corners of the room as 'I strongly agree', 'I strongly disagree', 'I agree somewhat', and 'I'm not sure'. The children then choose a corner to move to a corner in response to a statement or question.	**'Analogies'** In classrooms with older children, children can be challenged to work in pairs to come up with an analogy that explains their learning. The appropriateness of the analogy can illustrate how much they have understood of the lesson.
'Learning walk' This can be used for peer or self-assessment. For self-assessment, it involves the children moving around the room, looking at each others' work. They use what they have seen to then identify a strength and an area to develop in their own work.	**'Learning walk'** This can be used for peer or self-assessment. For peer assessment, it involves the children laying their work out on the table. The children move around the room, looking at each others' work. They choose one or two pieces to assess, writing their comments on a sticky note and leaving it on the work. *Also see Case study 4.2.*
'3-2-1-Go!' This is often an end-of-lesson plenary. The children identify three things they learned from the lesson, two things they want to know more about, and one question they have about the learning.	**'Present and ask'** The children present their own work to the class or a group, who can then ask questions to explore the learning further. *Also see below.*

Two approaches to structuring peer assessment are 'Two stars and a wish' or a 'Feedback sandwich'. The former involves the children using the criteria set to identify two strengths in the work (the stars) and one aspect to develop (the wish); the latter is similar but sandwiches the aspect to develop between two strengths. Children can find such feedback generic unless there is precise criteria to support the development of more purposeful precise comments – for example, responses such as 'It's good' or 'Write better sentences' can become 'The adverb made the sentence more interesting' or 'More adverbs could make it even more interesting'. The key here is the understanding that the feedback has a precise focus designed to support learning and is guided by specific criteria. The feedback should be a *recipe for action* (Wiliam, 2018).

CASE STUDY 4.1 SELF-ASSESSMENT AS PART OF THE LESSON

Stoberry Park Primary School

Stoberry Park Primary School uses self-assessment in most lessons and this is centred on clear success criteria that link to the learning objective. The learning objective is defined as 'We Are Learning To . . .', or 'WALT', and the success criteria as 'What I'm Looking For . . .', or 'WILF', and the latter sets out the key learning in the lesson that the children are trying to achieve in order to meet the objective. Space is provided for the children to assess their learning against each criteria. The criteria are clear and focused, allowing for the child to understand expectations of learning throughout the lesson, as well as identify what aspects of their learning they are assessing. The written WILF criteria allow the teacher to co-assess the learning, highlighting in green the criteria the child has evidenced.

The child's response can take different forms – for example, they could colour the box red, amber or green depending on their assessment of their learning. This is often known as using 'traffic lights'. Alternatively, they could draw an emoji – i.e. a happy face, neutral face or sad face – for each criteria. Regardless of the child's written response, it is the use of the criteria to guide the self-assessment that is key.

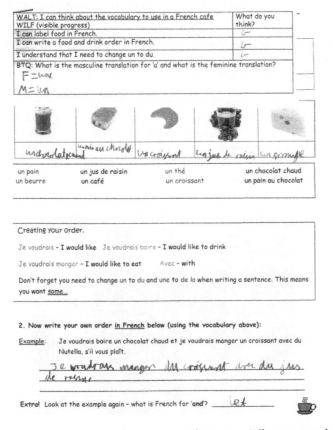

Figure 4.1   Self-assessment in a French lesson

CASE STUDY 4.2 PEER ASSESSMENT IN ACTION

Shaw Primary School

At Shaw Primary School, group talk and peer assessment were key features of science lessons. For example, in a Year 5 space lesson a whole-class carpet discussion about the Earth and Sun was followed by the pupils working in pairs or threes, using balls to physically model the orbit of the Earth around the Sun. As the children moved the Earth ball, they gave a commentary on what was happening, which was then peer assessed for clarity and accuracy. The groups gave advice to each other on how to improve their explanations. The teacher emphasised that they should aim to use scientific vocabulary accurately, which led to the pupils listening for the words 'orbit' or 'axis' in the explanations.

While in a Year 4 lesson on classification, the children worked in threes to create a branching key to sort animals by writing yes/no questions on sticky notes. The pupils had struggled with keys in the previous lesson and the teacher used this information formatively to adapt her planning in order to revisit the task. After partner discussions to raise questions (e.g. 'Does it have four legs?', 'Does it eat meat?'), the children were asked to self-assess their confidence in making a branching key; this was used formatively to create mixed-confidence groups. Peer assessment was then used formatively during a mini-plenary in the middle of the lesson, when pupils were asked to do a 'learning walk' around the classroom, to look at each other's keys and to pick out elements of a successful key before returning to improve their own key.

Both lessons featured explicit criteria, which supported reliability of pupil and teacher judgements. In the Year 4 lesson, the class constructed the success criteria for what constituted an effective branching key within the lesson. In the Year 5 lesson, the children made suggestions for the features of a successful explanation of the Earth's orbit.

In both lessons, peer assessment was used formatively by the pupils in the monitoring of their learning: the pupils were asked to peer assess each other's work and provide feedback; they had time to act on that feedback to improve their modelling or keys. The use of feedback within the lesson was significant because it made the assessment fully formative; the pupils were *activated as resources for each other* (Wiliam, 2018). The timely feedback and improvement also made the formative assessment manageable within the lesson.

Figure 4.2   Peer assessment to support explanations of the Earth's orbit of the Sun

CHILDREN'S PERCEPTIONS OF THEIR ROLE IN FORMATIVE ASSESSMENT

By giving due regard to children's perceptions, children may eventually become increasingly motivated to challenge themselves independently, as they may move from perceiving any mistakes as failures (Ryan and Deci, 2000), instead viewing them as opportunities for learning. Therefore, it is important to consider the perspectives and views of the children in the assessment process. It does not always follow that approaches the teacher feels are effective are viewed in the same way by the children, so exploring their perspectives can support an assessment process in which they are motivated to engage. A discussion of the views of four children is provided in Case study 4.3.

CASE STUDY 4.3 CHILDREN'S PERCEPTIONS OF SELF- AND PEER ASSESSMENT

Leo, Jenna, Wills and Chloe

There are a number of influences of other ideas and concepts that children hold that can affect their engagement with the peer-assessment process. For example, Leo (age 9) explained that he thinks that looking at someone else's work is 'cheating' and that others want to copy his work rather than assess it. As a result, he deliberately completes his work incorrectly so it cannot be copied. This brings us back to the concept of trust in the assessment process and in the person giving feedback. As considered earlier in the chapter, clarity over the purpose of the assessments and precise criteria can help to mitigate these misconceptions, encouraging children to view the assessment as a constructive process; children need to trust that the activity is for their benefit, and that their work is theirs alone. This is an example of the relational view of learning in that *the interaction of all elements in the situation* (Miller and Lavin, 2007) are considered.

Jenna (age 8) and Chloe (age 7) view the concept of peer assessment as helpful, as having 'another pair of eyes' can help them to see areas to develop in their work, but they agree that they place a greater value on assessment that is founded on clear assessment criteria; 'self-assessment is useful as long as there is success criteria . . . and a checklist of things that should be included'. This reflects the aforementioned need for precise and concise criteria from which the children can assess. It is essential that this is common practice in every assessment activity; Wills (age 10) stated: 'I don't get valuable feedback', so considers peer-assessment activities to be 'rubbish'. The engagement of pupils in the process is vital, so teachers need to ensure that children understand how to make the process valuable.

This is also the case for self-assessment, where children can have difficulty identifying areas to improve in their own work; as Chloe (age 11) noted: 'If I think it's fine, then I'm not going to find anything wrong with it.' Therefore, the children need to be clear about what specifically they look for and how to recognise if it needs to be improved. Wills's experience of self-assessment activities are those that set clear criteria from which to assess, and he therefore thinks this approach 'helps you to see what you can do better'.

The children were all in agreement that 'If there's not enough time or I'm not sure of how to do it, it's a waste of time'. Therefore, in addition to regular modelling of the process and clarity around what specifically to assess being important supports for children, allocating sufficient time to engage is an essential component that indicates that the process and their efforts are of value.

CLASSROOM CULTURE AND EFFECTIVE QUESTIONING TO SUPPORT PEER ASSESSMENT

The use of questioning in the peer-assessment process can be daunting as children want to feel competent in front of their peers. Planning for and modelling effective questioning that supports, encourages and extends learning is ideally a continuous and embedded process in primary classrooms. Through the careful consideration of questioning in all lessons, a learning environment that encourages and fosters questioning as a tool to enhance learning and understanding can begin to develop, along with a growing sense that asking questions is an integral aspect of learning. Therefore, the need to appear competent or to please the teacher can be mitigated by the supportive, learning-focused environment, where mistakes are celebrated as opportunities to learn rather than as an indication of incompetence on the part of the child or disappointment on the part of the teacher. Issues arise here around intrinsic versus extrinsic motivation for children to engage and succeed in their learning, which will not be explored in this chapter, but which are influencing factors that teachers should also consider when seeking to establish such an environment.

Cowie (2005) determined that children can be reluctant to ask questions, assuming that they are alone in not understanding learning and their peers ask questions from a knowledgeable position. Therefore, clarity around the purpose of questioning can support the development of an assessment culture that fosters learning and values constructive feedback, viewing it as a positive rather than a judgement or criticism. A structured peer dialogue centred around the learning focus can be an effective approach to peer assessment if there are carefully built-in questions for the children to ask. Again, the criteria need to be precise and concise for this to be a learning focused activity – for example, in an art lesson the children may assess the use of colour and lines after drawing a self-portrait in the style of Vincent van Gogh. In this lesson, children could 'present and ask'. In this activity, the children present their own work to the class or a group, who can then ask questions to explore the learning further. A well-known example of seeking and applying peer feedback is 'Austin's butterfly', where Austin repeatedly acts on specific guidance to make dramatic improvements to his observational drawing (EL Education, 2019). The discussion of work allows children to explain their reasoning to their peers, providing the opportunity for shared understanding. Again, this is a co-construction of knowledge for the questioners and the presenter; both are developing their knowledge through the process.

How children view themselves *affects the degree to which they engage in learning* (Robinson and Fielding, 2007) and this self-view is affected by the relationships that children develop in the classroom. Therefore, a culture of respect and trust, creating a safe space for learning and assessment, is an essential component of the classroom. In addition, social relations impact on the accuracy of peer assessment (Harris and Brown, 2013), with some children feeling uncomfortable telling their peers where they have not met the criteria or with others knowing about their work. Feedback from a close friend may be deemed trustworthy or may lead to worries about damaging the friendship (Fong et al., 2018, p6). As such, the approach to the implementation of peer-assessment activities requires careful consideration of the pairings or groupings, ensuring that the process is built on a foundation of support for the development of skills in giving and receiving constructive feedback. The accessibility of written work may also need to be taken into account, with children needing to be able to read their peers' feedback in order to respond accordingly.

Peer assessment is a complex social activity that needs to be scaffolded and developed over time. It is important to ensure that children move from supported peer assessment to independent peer assessment at a pace that is appropriate for them, and that this is mirrored in the use of self-assessment. This highlights the importance of using peer and self-assessment regularly. Literature (Noonan and Duncan, 2005; Panadero and Brown, 2017) supports children's assertions that they find peer assessment in particular is 'rarely used'. This means that they may not have sufficient opportunity to refine their skills in understanding the purpose and value of peer assessment, offering and receiving constructive feedback, and developing a culture of trust and respect that facilitates effective engagement with and in the process. Therefore, incorporating peer assessment as a regular component of lessons can address this, while ensuring that its use is purposeful, deliberate and tailored to the learning in the lesson. The previously explored scaffolding and support that can be put in place for children to learn how to give and receive constructive feedback throughout the peer-assessment process can add value, supporting the development of skills that improve the quality of the feedback given. These are examples of the transferable skills that the children need to develop in order for self-assessment to be equally effective.

Table 4.3   Peer and self-assessment in the classroom: a summary of key messages

- A *classroom culture* that embraces mistakes as opportunities to learn should be encouraged.
- Children's assessments should be *explicitly recognised* as having value for the overall assessment of progress and attainment.
- Assessment activities should be *purposefully designed* to enhance the learning in the lesson.
- Assessment activities should *consider the social dynamic* in the classroom.
- Criteria children use to assess should *centre around the learning focus*.
- Criteria should be *clear, precise and concise*.
- Approaches to assessment should be *regularly modelled* and *continually evident* in a range of lessons.
- Children should have *support to develop* their skill set - for example, using prompts before working independently.
- Feedback should *respond to the work* rather than the child.
- The assessment process should be *monitored by the teacher*.

CONCLUSION

Peer and self-assessment are complex activities that can be affected by the classroom culture, relationships with peers, confidence and perceived value of the process. They demand a specific skill set in both giving and receiving constructive feedback that supports learning and motivates the learner to respond, and this skill set can be supported, facilitated and enhanced through the careful and deliberate design of purposeful activities. Teachers' awareness of their own assumptions in terms of the skills that children possess for participation in peer assessment effectively and purposefully can help to ensure that children are regularly given the opportunities to acquire and practise these skills. Clear assessment criteria and a classroom culture that embraces errors as opportunities for learning can lead to children experiencing peer- and self-assessment activities that are valuable and worthwhile processes that enhance their learning.

REFERENCES

Boaler, J (2000) Mathematics from another world: traditional communities and the alienation of learners. *Journal of Mathematical Behavior, 18*: 379–97.

Bozkurt, E and Demir, R (2013) Students' views on peer assessment: a case study. *Ilkogretim Online, 12*(1): 241–53.

Cowie, B (2005) Student views of Assessment for Learning: (alias formative assessment). *New Zealand Science Teacher*, (110): 15–17.

Crichton, H and McDaid, A (2016) Learning intentions and success criteria: learners' and teachers' views. *Curriculum Journal, 27*(2): 190.

Education Endowment Foundation (EEF) (2018) *Metacognition and Self-regulated Learning: Guidance Report.* London: EEF.

EL Education (2019) Austin's Butterfly Drafts: models of excellence. Available online at: https://modelsof excellence.eleducation.org/projects/austins-butterfly-drafts (last accessed 22.1.19).

Foley, S (2013) Student views of peer assessment at the International School of Lausanne. *Journal of Research in International Education, 12*(3): 201–13.

Fong, CJ, Schallert, DL, Williams, KM, Williamson, ZH, Warner, JR, Lin, S and Kim, YW (2018) When feedback signals failure but offers hope for improvement: a process model of constructive criticism. *Thinking Skills and Creativity, 30*: 42–53.

Harlen, W and Qualter, A (2018) *The Teaching of Science in Primary Schools* (7th edn). New York: Routledge, 240–50.

Harris, LR and Brown, GTL (2013) Opportunities and obstacles to consider when using peer- and self-assessment to improve student learning: case studies into teachers' implementation. *Teaching and Teacher Education, 36*: 101–11.

Miller, D and Lavin, F (2007) 'But now I feel I want to give it a try': formative assessment, self-esteem and a sense of competence. *Curriculum Journal, 18*(1): 3–25.

Noonan, B and Duncan, CR (2005) Peer and self-assessment in high schools. *Practical Assessment, Research & Evaluation, 10*(17).

Panadero, E and Brown, GTL (2017) Teachers' reasons for using peer assessment: positive experience predicts use. *European Journal of Psychology of Education, 32*(1): 133–56.

Pellegrino, J, Chudowsky, N and Glaser, R (eds) (2001) *Knowing what students know: The science and design of educational assessment.* Washington, DC: National Academy Press.

Robinson, C and Fielding, M (2007) Children and their primary schools: pupils' voices. *Primary Review Research Briefings 5/3*, Cambridge: University of Cambridge Faculty of Education.

Rudduck, J, Chaplain, R and Wallace, C (1996) *School Improvement: What Can Pupils Tell Us?* London: David Fulton.

Ryan, RM and Deci, EL (2000) Self-determination theory and the facilitation of intrinsic motivation, social development, and well-being. *American Psychologist, 55*(1): 68–78.

Smith, PM and Hackling, MW (2016) Supporting teachers to develop substantive discourse in primary science classrooms. *Australian Journal of Teacher Education, 41*(4).

Wiliam, D (2018) *Embedded Formative Assessment* (2nd edn). Bloomington, IN: Solution Tree.

5

SUMMATIVE USE OF ASSESSMENT

DARREN MCKAY AND SARAH EARLE

— PURPOSE OF THIS CHAPTER

In this chapter we will:

- develop an understanding of summative assessment, including key terms in this field;

- explore statutory summative assessment and reporting arrangements;

- examine how summative assessments may be used in schools to support pupil progress and transition.

INTRODUCTION

An assessment is used summatively when it provides a judgement, score, description or summary regarding attainment at a particular point in time. Summative judgements could be the result of, for example, observation of children performing in a particular task; assessing a piece or pieces of work; informal and formal testing; or a summary of work across the term. Such information can be reported to pupils, parents, other teachers, senior leaders, governors, inspectors or government.

Summative assessment is often portrayed as the poor relation to formative assessment, with researchers emphasising the positive impact of formative assessment on children's learning, contrasted with the negative impact of 'high stakes' summative assessment (Mansell et al., 2009; Gardner et al., 2010). However, much summative assessment in primary schools does not need to be 'high stakes'. This chapter will explore how teachers can make the best use of summative assessment in the primary classroom.

WHY IS SUMMATIVE ASSESSMENT IMPORTANT FOR TEACHERS?

Summative assessment can provide a summary of what a child has learnt at a given point in time, usually towards the end of a unit of work (Harris and Lowe, 2018; Briggs, 2019). A numerical value, adjective or description may be used to give the assessment data meaning so the information can be shared with, and understood by, others (see Chapter 7 for how this data is used). This is valuable information for teachers, which can be used to benefit the children they teach.

Summative assessment can be seen as an integral part of the curriculum and, when used effectively, will help to define the future learning of the children. By analysing an end-of-term assessment, you can identify areas of difficulty for individuals and groups in your class, helping you to plan for the subsequent term. As Harlen (2018, p197) suggests, summative assessment should be used to *help learning but in the longer term and in a less direct way than in the case of formative assessment*. This longer term view can extend to a later cohort of children, as you annotate your plans for the following year – for example, noting to yourself to try a different order for the introduction of concepts the following year. Receiving summative assessment data from a previous teacher provides useful information to support planning for your new class, as discussed more fully below in the section on transition.

One purpose of summative assessment, which has grown in recent years, is its accountability function. It is important that teachers understand the uses to which assessment data is put, in order to decide what is appropriate for their classrooms. Summative assessment has been used to hold schools to account, with results becoming 'high stakes' when they are used for target setting and the ranking of schools. After the replacement of the levels system in England with age-related expectations, the Commission on Assessment without Levels, chaired by John McIntosh (2015), published a report containing numerous recommendations relating to assessment practice in schools. Significantly, the report made clear distinctions between the ways in which assessment for summative purposes should be used.

1. In-school summative assessment: enabling schools to evaluate how much a pupil has learned at the end of a teaching period – e.g. *End of year exams, Short end of topic or unit tests, Reviews for pupils with SEN and disabilities.*

2. Statutory summative assessment: used by the government to hold schools to account – e.g. *National Curriculum tests at the end of Key Stage 2; National Curriculum teacher assessments at the end of Key Stage 1.*

(McIntosh, 2015, p18)

This clear distinction between school-based and statutory assessment acknowledges the importance of both uses of summative assessment. End of Key Stage statutory assessment is an expectation, but schools should also be using school-based summative assessments to monitor pupil progress. Pupil progress will be considered in more detail from the classroom perspective in Chapter 6 and from the whole-school perspective in Chapter 7.

IS SUMMATIVE ASSESSMENT MORE THAN A TEST?

One of the most frequent examples of assessment used for summative purposes is a test. This may be a spelling test taken in class each week, a statutory test produced by the government or a bicycle proficiency test. All of these are summative assessments of what the learner can or cannot do at a given time – i.e. while they are sitting the test. Tests are relatively easy to administer and can be quick to mark. A whole cohort can sit the test at once, which makes this form of summative assessment appear cost-effective. It is no wonder that tests have become so popular as an assessment tool, despite concerns about curriculum narrowing and their use with younger children.

However, summative assessment is not limited to testing. When a teacher reviews a sample of several pieces of a child's independent writing, they are able to build a picture of the child as a writer: a summary of the child's strengths and areas to improve. This is an assessment with a summative purpose. Assessment criteria can be used to support the teacher to translate their opinion about the child's writing into a statement that can be recorded and referred to later, by the teacher or other interested parties. By applying an agreed set of criteria to the judgement, the teacher is using a common language of assessment that others can understand. This assessment can then be used in a more reliable way as all the interested parties can refer to the criteria, which will give a picture of the child as a learner, without the need to read the child's writing themselves. It is important to note the flaws in any assessment. In this case, the interpretation of the criteria is open to personal bias in judgement or misunderstanding. Criteria may be somewhat broad and difficult to apply, or may not truly reflect the work sampled. Moderation and standardisation meetings are one way to reduce this difference in judgements so that at least the group of people who attended the moderation/standardisation meeting can agree how the criteria relates to the work sampled. Chapter 8 discusses the process of moderation, and we will explore validity and reliability in more detail below.

TYPES OF SUMMATIVE ASSESSMENTS

Harlen (2018) suggests that summative and formative assessments are not different types of assessment but rather assessment used in a different way, for a different purpose. This means that any assessment information can be used summatively. For example, judgements of 'meeting' age-related expectations can arise from end of Key Stage mathematics test scores or from the collation of observations of children in the Early Years portfolio (discussed further below). These two examples draw on very different data sets: the test scores result from performance at a particular point in time, a 'snapshot' summative assessment, while the portfolio draws on a wide range of activities over an extended period – a 'summary' summative assessment.

Returning to the key principles of validity and reliability, which were introduced in Chapter 2, snapshot and summary assessments have different strengths. Snapshot assessments can be more reliable, because they can be taken under similar conditions and mark schemes can create high levels of consistency between markers. This makes snapshot assessments, like standardised tests, useful for comparisons across schools and cohorts. However, snapshots are exactly that – information about a small part of the curriculum at a particular point in time, which may make them less valid measures than is widely assumed. By asking different questions on a different day, many pupils would receive a different result (Newton, 2009), so while snapshots may be higher on reliability, it needs to be remembered that they do not provide a full picture of a pupil's attainment.

Summary judgements can also be explored through the lens of reliability and validity. Summaries can draw on a wide range of information from the primary classroom, providing a more complete sampling of the curriculum, making them potentially more valid summative assessments. This is particularly true when considering the difficulties in using standardised testing with young children, a topic currently being debated with the planned introduction of Early Years baseline measures. However, the principle of reliability is more problematic for summary judgements, since it is harder to ensure a consistency of judgements over a wide range of activities. Asking yourself the reliability question of whether other teachers would agree with your judgement is dependent on whether the other teachers have as much information about each context and activity as you do. This is where exemplification and moderation for professional learning are invaluable, as will be discussed in Chapter 8.

Useful for both snapshot and summary assessments is a clear set of statements, which are used to support a judgement about a learner's performance. Such statements could be in the form of end-of-unit expectations, National Curriculum descriptors or a Teacher Assessment Framework (e.g. STA, 2018). It is important to clarify whether the assessment judgement being made requires a 'best fit' or a 'secure fit'. 'Best fit' judgements require the majority of criteria to be achieved, as in the previous system of levels, while 'secure fit' judgements require all the criteria to be achieved, as was first introduced for the system of age-related expectations. The 'secure fit' is problematic if there are pupils who, for example, overall produce good writing outcomes, but may have not included a particular element, or may have a specific difficulty with handwriting or spelling. This issue led to the latest guidance for teacher assessment of writing in England, which takes a more flexible approach and allows teacher discretion for particular weaknesses (STA, 2018).

Criterion-referenced assessment provides a shared language for summative assessment and can support the reliability of judgements, alongside moderation and exemplification. However, such lists of criteria can become unwieldy and narrow the curriculum to a 'tick-box' culture (Mansell et al., 2009). Criteria lists can be supportive, but if the focus is too tight on minute details, the bigger picture may be missed, as has been noted above in the assessment of writing. Some schools are now exploring 'comparative judgement' (Christodoulou, 2016) as a way to make judgements about writing without relying on extensive criteria lists. The shared criteria are still present, but in a more holistic sense, as the teachers judge pairs of work samples. With large numbers of teachers doing these pairs comparisons online, reliability is enhanced without adversely affecting the individual workload of the teacher.

Decisions about whether an assessment is fit for purpose also includes consideration of its consequences. For example, test preparation may lead to skewing of the curriculum towards the easily tested information, *a negative wash-back into teaching and learning* (Green and Oates, 2009, p231). When this happens, teachers and senior leaders should discuss whether the purpose and use of the assessment merits such changes to curriculum provision.

SUMMATIVE ASSESSMENTS TO AGE 11

Children are assessed from the moment they are born. These early assessments are important, and are used in a summative and diagnostic way to check that a child is developing as expected. If not, action is taken by the range of healthcare professionals involved in a child's early life.

Between the ages of 2 and 11, a variety of summative assessments are made on a child to record a snapshot of their learning achievements. These can be used to support the child's learning, but may also be used to hold schools to account, and, by default teachers to account – the statutory summative assessments referred to by McIntosh (2015) above. Table 5.1 below illustrates the range of summative assessments completed, the main audience and how each could be used. The 2–2½ years' review has been included, as this is the first time for many children that the assessments outcomes are shared with education staff.

Table 5.1   Major summative assessment points for a child aged 2–11 in England

Assessment	Completed by	Audience	Potential uses
2–2½ years' review	Parent Health Visitor (HV)	Health Visitor Team EYFS staff	• Summative assessment of child's development at 24 to 30 months • Opportunity for parents to ask questions • Opportunity for HV to give reassurance and signpost support • EYFS staff review checks during home visits or induction sessions
Foundation Stage Profile (FSP)	FS2 teacher	Government Ofsted LA/MAT Leadership in school Year 1 staff Parents Child	• Summative assessment of child's development and learning at end of EYFS • Baseline assessment for entry into KS1 • Identify strengths and areas for development • Used to measure progress made from EYFS to end of KS1
Phonics screening	Year 1 staff Year 2 staff	Government Ofsted LA/MAT Leadership in school Year 1 staff Year 2 staff Parents Child	• Summative assessment of child's phonological awareness • Identify those who need additional support to achieve pass mark • Hold staff/school to account • Review of phonics curriculum within school
End of Key Stage 2	Year 6 staff	Government Ofsted LA/MAT Leadership in school Primary school staff Year 7 staff Parents Child	• Summative assessment of child's achievement in reading, writing, maths and science • Identify those who need additional support • Setting/streaming for Year 7 • Hold staff/school to account • Review of curriculum within school

HOW IS SUMMATIVE ASSESSMENT USED WITHIN AND BEYOND THE CLASSROOM?

Chapter 7 includes an overview of how the National Curriculum has changed in response to assessment used for summative purposes. Teachers and leaders in schools also use summative assessment, in the medium to long term, to monitor and review their school's curriculum. Decisions are made regarding the amount of time given to a subject or the way in which subjects are taught. Questions are asked, such as 'Should we teach subjects in a discrete way or use an interdisciplinary approach to organise the children's learning experiences?' Many schools adopt a combination of discrete subjects (usually English, maths and PE), and thematic topics that incorporate science and/or foundation subjects.

Summative assessments are used by class teachers to give a snapshot or summary of how their pupils are progressing, noting whether the children have learnt what the teacher intended them to learn and to what extent. Armed with this information, the teacher can then decide if they can continue to teach the next sequence of learning or if a sequence of learning needs to be repeated, albeit in an adapted manner. This process could be seen as using summative assessment in a formative way, although, as stated previously, summative assessment can be used to inform curriculum development in the medium to long term.

Schools report children's achievement to parents during meetings or in written reports. Reports could include a summative description of the child as a learner, clearly detailing the child's achievements, strengths and areas for development. Less useful for parents are reports in which children's learning is reduced to percentages, scores, grades or numbers that have little meaning outside the confines of the educational profession.

Within schools, colleagues share summative assessments at the end of a school year or Key Stage. A commentary often accompanies the assessment data to explain and define what has been taught, what has been learnt and what still needs to be taught. Such reports or data summaries may be explicitly related to the criteria of the key outcomes or goals stipulated within the National Curriculum, but not limited to it. The assessment criteria are the expected level of attainment at a given point in a child's learning and may apply to a single year group, or two or more year groups. Most recently in England, these have been called 'age-related expectations'. Transition will be discussed further below, with an example of passing information from Reception to Year 1.

School leaders use the summative assessment data to hold teachers to account. Governors, local authorities and Multi-Academy Trust leaders use the school data to hold school leaders to account. McKay (2019) discusses how this accountability changes as a teacher progresses in their career. The use of data will be the main focus of discussion in Chapter 7.

In England, English and maths summative assessments have been viewed by many as more important than the assessment of other areas of the curriculum. A contributing factor in this is the pressure that many school leaders feel under by the introduction of league tables in 1992 by the UK government. By focusing developments on the quality of teaching and learning, raising standards in the achievement of the children in English and maths, a positive impact should be observed in the school's position in the league tables. All school leaders want their children to improve and make progress in English and maths, but many do not want that at the expense of other subjects.

Many schools make summative assessments beyond the core curriculum. National Curriculum expectations are available to support these judgements, but schools may be more creative in the ways they use assessment of foundation subjects for summative purposes. EYFS practitioners work with children and parents to capture significant learning through the use of photos, observation notes and samples of children's outcomes (see Case study 5.1 and 8.1). These are combined, often in a chronological sequence to record the story of the child as a learner. Sketchbooks are often used in primary phases as a record of the child's development in art (see Case study 6.1). At specific times over the year, the child, their peers and their teachers can annotate their work to capture a summary of the child's learning. Children can create posters, projects, artefacts and dioramas, individually or in groups, to demonstrate what they have learnt over the course of a unit of work. Such assessment can be made for summative purposes, linking to learning intentions for the unit, and used to record achievement.

IT can and does play a significant part in assessment used for summative purposes. Software can support both assessment of the learning (creating the data) and tracking (analysing the data). It is important to understand the difference between these two functions of the application or programme. IT can support the making of summative judgements by providing an efficient way of storing evidence, which may be linked to criteria, or by collating ongoing teacher judgements. Software that collates or aggregates judgements usually requires the highlighting of criteria and/or allocating a level of agreement with each criterion. The software will then analyse the inputs and produce a suggested summative assessment. This is usually in the form of a number or statement relating to the level of achievement expected for the stage in the child's learning. Most systems will allow the user to agree or disagree with the assessment and change it accordingly. Understanding the weighting given to different elements is useful when considering whether the suggested summative assessment is appropriate.

IT can be very useful as a tool for tracking, providing a way of recording assessment data and then using the software to perform/support interrogation and analysis of the data. The software can help to identify patterns and significant differences from the expected or norm. IT used to track and analyse data can be extremely efficient and will allow data to be manipulated quickly to focus on an individual, group or cohort (as discussed further in Chapter 7). When analysing data in this way, it is important to remember the origins of the data, to ensure that conclusions are in proportion to the trustworthiness of the data.

SUMMATIVE ASSESSMENT AT TRANSITION

Points of transition are a time when summative assessment is most useful for the teacher. When a child is changing class or school, the new teacher needs to know as much as possible about them to support their ongoing development. A summary of attainment, in the form of summative grades, statements or descriptions, may be passed to the new teacher in the form of a report or during a handover meeting. A particularly comprehensive transition process takes place in England when a 5-year-old child moves from the Early Years Foundation Stage (from a class called Reception or Foundation Stage 2) to Year 1 of Key Stage 1. The summative process is summarised below and then exemplified in Case study 5.1. A further EYFS example is provided in Chapter 8 when considering moderation processes.

EARLY YEARS FOUNDATION STAGE PROFILE

The Early Years Foundation Stage profile is a statutory summative assessment in England, which summarises children's attainment at age 5. Teachers use collated evidence from observations and activities across the year to make a judgement for every Early Learning Goal (see Table 5.2) and write a learning commentary (see Table 8.2).

Table 5.2   Early Learning Goals (ELG) for England (DfE, 2017)

Areas of learning and development	ELG areas	Example of ELG statement (judged as emerging, expected or exceeded for each child at the end of EYFS)
Communication and language	Listening and attention Understanding Speaking	Understanding: children follow instructions involving several ideas or actions. They answer 'how' and 'why' questions about their experiences and in response to stories or events.
Physical development	Moving and handling Health and self-care	Moving and handling: children show good control and co-ordination in large and small movements. They move confidently in a range of ways, safely negotiating space. They handle equipment and tools effectively, including pencils for writing.
Personal, social and emotional development	Self-confidence and self-awareness Managing feelings and behaviour Making relationships	Making relationships: children play co-operatively, taking turns with others. They take account of one another's ideas about how to organise their activity. They show sensitivity to others' needs and feelings, and form positive relationships with adults and other children.
Literacy	Reading Writing	Reading: children read and understand simple sentences. They use phonic knowledge to decode regular words and read them aloud accurately. They also read some common irregular words. They demonstrate understanding when talking with others about what they have read.
Mathematics	Numbers Shape, space and measures	Numbers: children count reliably with numbers from 1 to 20, place them in order and say which number is one more or one less than a given number. Using quantities and objects, they add and subtract two single-digit numbers and count on or back to find the answer. They solve problems, including doubling, halving and sharing.
Understanding the world	People and communities The world Technology	Technology: children recognise that a range of technology is used in places such as homes and schools. They select and use technology for particular purposes.
Expressive arts and design	Exploring and using media and materials Being imaginative	Being imaginative: children use what they have learnt about media and materials in original ways, thinking about uses and purposes. They represent their own ideas, thoughts and feelings through design and technology, art, music, dance, role-play and stories.

CASE STUDY 5.1 TRANSITION FROM EYFS TO KEY STAGE 1 IN A LARGE PRIMARY SCHOOL IN GREATER LONDON

The school is a three-form entry primary school within Greater London. There are 24 classes, ranging from Foundation Stage 1 (FS1) to Year 6. A senior teacher leads the Early Years Team with responsibility for the six classes in the Early Years Foundation Stage and the three classes in Year 1. Children join the school in groups over a three-week period. Week one is mornings, week two mornings and lunch, week three full days. Each child's induction is adapted to their individual needs, but most are settled by the end of week three. Parents are welcome to join the children for the initial part of the day in FS1 (also known as Nursery). This practice is encouraged throughout the first year at the school, but is one that most families stop before Christmas. Summative baseline assessments are made on each child once they are settled and before the end of the first six weeks in school. At the end of the child's EYFS, the Foundation Stage Profile (FSP) is completed by the Foundation Stage 2 (FS2, also known as Reception) staff. This information is shared with the child, their parents and the Year 1 staff.

The FS2 and Year 1 teachers meet to discuss individual children's learning behaviours, attainment, friendship groups and any concerns the FS2 staff may have. This meeting is much like a pupil progress review meeting (see Chapter 6), but with a strong emphasis on the child's social and emotional development. Targets, based on the FSP summative assessments, are agreed for reading, writing and maths, and recorded on the school's database. The targets are shared with the children and parents. A parent year-group meeting at the start of Year 1 is held so that parents are clear about what to expect in Year 1. A booklet with the Year 1 Age Related Expectations (AREs) is distributed and explained during this meeting. The KS1 phonics screening is also explained and how parents can support their children.

Initially, the Year 1 team adopt the pedagogies and curriculum provision of FS2. Over a period of four to six weeks, depending on the summative assessment data of the FSP, the curriculum becomes more formal in the mornings with distinct lessons for English (including phonics) and maths. The afternoons remain more embedded in EYFS practice until Christmas, or earlier, depending on the cohort's needs.

CASE STUDY 5.2 'FORMATIVE TO SUMMATIVE' ASSESSMENT

In practical subjects like primary science, it is difficult to capture attainment in all areas – for example, to assess the skills of working scientifically with pencil and paper activities. Thus, summative assessment judgements need to draw on a wider range of activities (e.g. Figure 5.1). The Teacher Assessment in Primary Science (TAPS) project is based at Bath Spa University and funded by the Primary Science Teaching Trust. TAPS has developed a pyramid-shaped model to support teachers to use classroom activities to inform their summative judgements. Figure 5.2 shows the overall structure of the approach; further detail and exemplification can be found on the TAPS website (see reference below).

The base layers of the TAPS pyramid encapsulate formative assessment processes, which includes the active involvement of pupils (Chapter 4) and responsiveness of teachers (Chapter 3). Where there is a clear focus or clear criteria for an activity, the assessment information can be used formatively to support next steps, and then summatively to contribute to a summative summary (Earle et al., 2018). The arrow on the pyramid symbolises this flow of information. Summarising from a wide range of contexts supports validity because it samples a wide range of the curriculum. Clear criteria, exemplification and moderation discussions all contribute to enhanced reliability of summative judgements because they build a shared understanding of the subject.

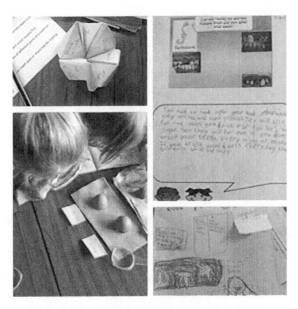

Figure 5.1   *Summative judgements can draw on assessment information from a range of activities – example from unit on teeth*

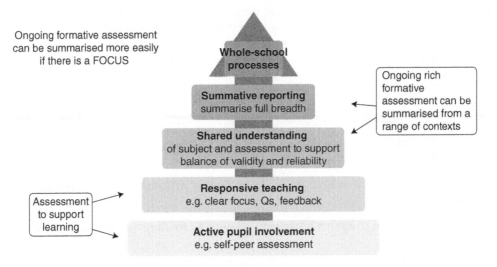

Figure 5.2   *Key principles of the TAPS pyramid model*

There is no set way of evidencing and collating the ongoing assessment information into a summative summary or judgement, since teachers and schools find different processes manageable for them, depending on the age of the pupils, the context and the assessment processes for other subjects. For example, teachers of younger children may create floorbooks for groups or the class in which they note down observations, while teachers of older children may use pupil books as a record

(Continued)

(Continued)

of progress through the topics. Other methods include annotating planning or highlighting curriculum coverage, noting those who have not yet met the objective; or group/class records on paper or electronically which are updated at significant points. For this to be a whole-school process, it is important for teachers to know which parts of the curriculum are unlikely to be covered in later years, so that attainment in these areas is passed on to the next class teacher.

CONCLUSION

Summative assessment is as much a part of a child's education as formative assessment, thus it is important to put it to good use. It has a vital roll in the medium- and long-term development of both the individual pupils and the school curriculum, at school and national levels.

It should be recognised that the use of summative assessment to hold schools to account can have significant impact on both staff working in schools and the children they teach. As part of being a primary teacher today, we must recognise the important role that summative assessment has and also the negative impact it may have on staff, children and parents. A question for you to ask is, 'How do we support the well-being of our children who may be in the frontline of a high-stakes context?' An essential step to achieve this is to remember that at the centre of all this assessment is a child with many skills, interests and attributes that need to be celebrated and acknowledged. The assessments that we complete are only one element of this and, of course, one that we want all children to do their very best at – but they are not the only reason that children go to school.

REFERENCES

Briggs, M (2019) 'What is assessment?'. In Carden, C (ed.) *Primary Teaching: Learning and Teaching in Primary Schools Today*. London: Teaching Matters, pp. 279–97.

Christodoulou, D (2016) *Making Good Progress? The Future of Assessment for Learning*. Oxford: Oxford University Press.

Department for Education (DfE) (2017) *Statutory Framework for the Early Years Foundation Stage*. London: DfE.

Earle, S, Qureshi, A, Rodger, P and Sampey, S (2018) Supporting assessment across school. In Serret, N and Earle, S (eds) *ASE Guide to Primary Science Education* (4th edn). Hatfield: Association for Science Education.

Gardner, J, Harlen, W, Hayward, L, Stobart, G, with Montgomery, M (2010) *Developing Teacher Assessment*. Maidenhead: Open University Press.

Green, S and Oates, T (2009) Considering the alternatives to national assessment arrangements in England: possibilities and opportunities. *Educational Research*, 51(2): 229–45.

Harlen, W with Qualter, A (2018) *The Teaching of Science in Primary Schools*. Abingdon: Routledge.

Harris, K and Lowe, S (2018) Assessment. In Cooper, H and Elton-Chalcraft, S (eds) *Professional Studies in Primary Education* (3rd edn). London: SAGE, pp. 96–120.

Mansell, W, James, M and the Assessment Reform Group (2009) *Assessment in Schools: Fit for Purpose?* London: Teaching and Learning Research Programme.

McIntosh, J (Chair) (2015) *Final Report of the Commission on Assessment without Levels.* Crown copyright.

McKay, D (2019) Is data the whole story? The data-led accountability of teachers. In Carden, C (ed.) *Primary Teaching: Learning and Teaching in Primary Schools Today.* London: Teaching Matters, pp. 425–41.

Newton, P. (2009) The reliability of results from national curriculum testing in England. *Educational Research, 51*(2): 181–212.

Standards and Testing Agency (STA) (2018) *Teacher assessment frameworks at the end of key stage 2: for use from the 2018/19 academic year onwards.* London: STA.

TAPS website. Available online at: https://pstt.org.uk/resources/curriculum-materials/assessment (last accessed 29.1.19).

6

PUPIL PROGRESS AND PROGRESSION

EMILY ASBURY

┌─ **PURPOSE OF THIS CHAPTER** ─────────────────────────────────

In this chapter we will:

- explore how pupil progress is evidenced;

- develop an awareness of the different stakeholders in pupil progress;

- consider progression in different areas of the curriculum;

- examine progress in the Early Years and for children with additional needs.
└───

INTRODUCTION

The way in which progress is perceived influences classroom and whole-school approaches to teaching and learning; thus, it is important to understand the concept of pupil progress and how it is enacted in the primary classroom. This is also an area of assessment strongly linked to accountability and performance management, with pupil progress often used as a measure of how well both individual teachers and schools are performing.

Throughout this chapter, we will consider what progress is and what it looks like in practice. This chapter will also consider progression within different areas of the curriculum; how pupil progress is evidenced and how this might look in the Early Years and for pupils with Special Educational Needs and Disabilities (SEND). This chapter will be predominantly focused on pupil progress within the classroom, specifically how this is evidenced and the teacher's role in this process. In Chapter 7, you will find an exploration of pupil progress from a whole-school perspective, with consideration of the measurement and tracking of pupil data, together with an exploration of the way in which this data is used by school leaders.

WHAT DO WE MEAN BY PROGRESS?

'Pupil progress' relates to children's learning and the development that has been made, or is being made, towards an outcome or level of attainment. Commonly, pupil progress is considered in terms of working towards attainment targets or assessment points, sometimes called Age Related Expectations (AREs) or Age Related Goals (ARGs). Sean Harford, Ofsted's National Director of Education, states that,

By progress, we mean pupils knowing more and remembering more. Has a child really gained the knowledge to understand the key concepts and ideas? Is this enabling them to develop the skills they need to master? (Harford, 2018). Here, Harford suggests a distinction between progress and attainment, something we will explore in further detail later in the chapter. He suggests that progress can be considered in terms of knowledge and retention of information. It may therefore be useful to think of pupil progress as 'the stepping stones towards understanding a key concept or idea', or progress towards an attainment target or particular criteria. Tables 6.1 and 6.2 contain two examples to help clarify this further.

It is important to note that although discussions on pupil progress are often predominantly focused on formally assessed subjects such as English and maths, pupils make progress across the curriculum and within a range of different skills and contexts.

Table 6.1   *Indicators of pupil progress (English example)*

Attainment target	Age-related expectation	Indicators of pupil progress
The curriculum target that pupils are expected to know, apply and understand. This is the overall target of the teaching and learning and will be the focus of assessment.	*The curriculum attainment targets presented as assessment points and used as a focus for summative assessment. Commonly presented in 'child speak' to make them more accessible and allow for self-assessment.*	*The 'stepping stones' or individual elements required to reach and achieve the attainment target. A teacher can monitor the pupil's progress towards achieving a specific attainment target.*
Evaluate and edit (writing) by proposing changes to grammar and vocabulary to improve consistency, including the accurate use of pronouns in sentences. *Attainment target taken from National Curriculum for England (2013) (Year 3 and 4 programme of study – writing composition).*	I can improve my writing by changing grammar and vocabulary to improve consistency.	In order to reach the attainment target, a child will need to be able to: • read and check their own written work; • demonstrate an awareness of key grammatical features; • develop their vocabulary; • use a dictionary or thesaurus to support vocabulary choices; • be able to adapt their grammar choices and understand why they are doing so.

Table 6.2   *Indicators of pupil progress (geography example)*

Attainment target	Age-related expectation	Indicators of pupil progress
The curriculum target that pupils are expected to know, apply and understand. This is the overall target of the teaching and learning and will be the focus of assessment.	*The curriculum attainment targets presented as assessment points and used as a focus for summative assessment. Commonly presented in 'child speak' to make them more accessible and allow for self-assessment.*	*The 'stepping stones' or individual elements required to reach and achieve the attainment target. A teacher can monitor the pupil's progress towards achieving a specific attainment target.*

(Continued)

Table 6.2   (Continued)

Locate the world's countries, using maps to focus on Europe (including the location of Russia), and North and South America, concentrating on their environmental regions, key physical and human characteristics, countries, and major cities. *Attainment target taken from National Curriculum for England (2013) (Key Stage 2 programme of study – Geography, locational knowledge).*	I can locate the world's countries on a map or globe and talk about their key features and major cities.	In order to reach the attainment target, a child will need to be able to: • understand how to use a map or globe; • demonstrate an understanding of the different continents and land masses of the world; • develop an awareness of the differences between physical and human geography; • locate the major cities of the world.

PUPIL PROGRESS, ACHIEVEMENT AND ATTAINMENT: WHAT IS THE DIFFERENCE IN PRACTICE?

Progress, achievement and attainment were introduced in Chapter 2, but only in general terms, so we return to them here in order to discuss what they look like in classroom practice.

Attainment refers to the specific level or point that the child has reached at a certain time – for example, a child who is deemed to be 'meeting' at the end of Year 3 – whereas achievement takes into account the pupil's starting point, considering their attainment in context. For example, 'meeting' the age-related expectation could represent high achievement for a child whose prior attainment has been low, but low achievement for a child whose prior attainment has been high. Do note, however, that progress is not necessarily linear, with different children progressing at different rates at different times. We will consider this further in discussion of Figure 6.1.

Pupil progress also considers the children's starting point, but refers to the steps in learning towards standards or objectives. It has become particularly important for schools to demonstrate that gaps in learning are identified and addressed, with close monitoring of specific groups, such as children with pupil premium funding, to ensure that their needs are met. Some schools find it useful to consider 'expected' levels of progress, to help ensure that those with high prior attainment are being 'stretched'. Figure 6.1 provides an example of how that might look in practice for a school year without statutory testing. Although it is also important to remember that it is not possible to predict 'expected' progress accurately, since all children will mature and learn at different rates, such predictions can only be part of the information that is used to support a child to learn.

The dotted line indicating progress in Figure 6.1 is not a straight line, as progression is not linear – in fact, it could have been more up and down, flat or even dipped at certain points. Children who have a similar end point at the end of the school year may have had very different routes to get there. Some may have learnt

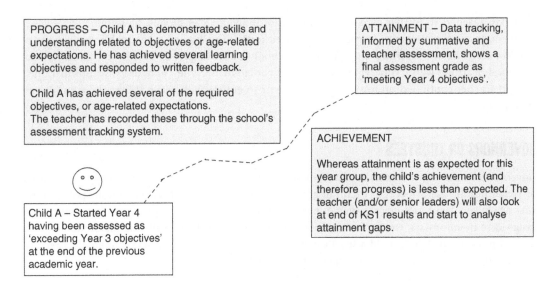

PROGRESS – Child A has demonstrated skills and understanding related to objectives or age-related expectations. He has achieved several learning objectives and responded to written feedback.

Child A has achieved several of the required objectives, or age-related expectations.
The teacher has recorded these through the school's assessment tracking system.

ATTAINMENT – Data tracking, informed by summative and teacher assessment, shows a final assessment grade as 'meeting Year 4 objectives'.

ACHIEVEMENT

Whereas attainment is as expected for this year group, the child's achievement (and therefore progress) is less than expected. The teacher (and/or senior leaders) will also look at end of KS1 results and start to analyse attainment gaps.

Child A – Started Year 4 having been assessed as 'exceeding Year 3 objectives' at the end of the previous academic year.

Figure 6.1   An example of progress, attainment and achievement

rapidly, then spent the rest of the year consolidating, others may have made steady progress, while yet others may have had a difficult year at home and found that maintaining last year's attainment was enough of a challenge. Pupil progress is likely to fluctuate for many different reasons, so it helps to understand each child's individual pathway in order to support them with the appropriate next step.

MONITORING PUPIL PROGRESS: WHO IS INVOLVED?

Different stakeholders in education will approach pupil progress in different ways and will therefore also have a different 'picture' of pupil progress according to how progress is reported to them and what they aim to 'do' with the data. Below is an overview of some of the key stakeholders in pupil progress.

TEACHERS

Teachers are responsible for the progress and overall attainment levels for all the children they teach, including those with special educational needs (as discussed below). Teacher practice is supported through discussion with colleagues and senior leaders, which may include pupil progress meetings. Pupil progress may be linked to teachers' performance-management targets. Teachers are also responsible for ensuring that additional adults in the classroom, including students, support pupil progress.

SENIOR LEADERSHIP TEAMS

The leadership teams within a school, and those within a wider federation or trust, will complete ongoing data tracking and analysis to monitor pupil progress and identify any gaps or underperforming groups. As part of this data tracking, school leadership teams may hold pupil progress meetings with class teachers to further explore the progress of individuals or groups, identifying strategies or interventions that can support learners, as discussed further in Chapter 7. Leadership teams will also monitor teaching and learning throughout the school – for example, by curriculum tracking, book scrutinies, learning walks, observations and pupil conferencing. They may use this information to support teacher continued professional development to ensure that staff training opportunities are appropriate.

GOVERNORS OR TRUSTEES

Governors or trustees will closely monitor the data of the school. This may take the form of a written or verbal headteacher's report at each full governing board meeting. There will also be points in the year where key data headlines are shared in more detail. One or several of the governors will also be assigned to monitor data; their role is to monitor and report on the overall data picture to all governors. Governors are able to hold a headteacher to account over data outcomes and are likely to also play a part in the performance management of that headteacher.

PARENTS

There will be several opportunities throughout the year for parents to engage in conversations about their children's progress. Most commonly, this will take place through parents' evenings or parent–teacher consultations. Data may also be shared on the reports that are sent to parents. There may be other opportunities for parents to come into school, such as parent assemblies or an open afternoon, to engage in conversations with their children or look at their books to gain additional insight into their progress. If a teacher has a specific concern or if a child has SEND, there are likely to be other formal meetings with parents throughout the school year.

SCHOOL INSPECTORS

The Office for Standards in Education, Children's Services and Skills (Ofsted) in England has a strong focus on pupil progress. Inspectors can gather evidence about the progress of current pupils in a variety of ways – for example, observations in lessons; discussions with pupils about their learning; and scrutiny of pupils' acquisition of knowledge, understanding and skills over time as shown in their work. Together with this, they will use the school's own information on pupil progress, taking account of the quality and rigour of the assessment on which it is based (Ofsted, 2018). At the time of writing, proposed changes to the Ofsted framework indicate a move away from focusing on headline data, to look instead at how schools are achieving these results, and whether they are offering a curriculum that is broad, rich and deep, or simply teaching to the test (DfE, 2018).

GOVERNMENT

The English government publishes school performance tables based on progress between the end of Key Stage 1 and the end of Key Stage 2. This is informed by both teacher assessment and test results, with the end of Key Stage 2 National Curriculum tests (SATs) giving a scaled score.

MAKING GOOD PROGRESS: WHAT CAN I DO?

Every teacher aims to support all pupils to make good progress in their lessons. A focus on pupil progress is also a statutory expectation for teachers. For example, in England the *Teachers' Standards* describe a responsibility to *promote good progress and outcomes by pupils* in Standard 2 (DfE, 2011), while in Scotland registered teachers are required to *ensure learning tasks are varied, differentiated and devised to build confidence and promote progress of all learners, providing effective support and challenge* (GTC for Scotland, 2012, p15). In Wales, the professional standard for pedagogy states: *The teacher consistently secures the best outcomes for learners through progressively refining teaching, influencing learners and advancing learning* (Welsh Government, 2017, p16). In Northern Ireland, statement 24 requires that *Teachers will: focus on assessment for learning by monitoring pupils' progress, giving constructive feedback to help pupils reflect on and improve their learning* (GTCNI, 2011, p15).

Primarily, you will ensure good progress for all children through responsive and reflective teaching. Strategies, such as effective assessment for learning, will support this by identifying gaps, enabling *learners and their teachers to decide where the learners are in their learning, where they need to go and how best to get there* (ARG, 2002). Table 6.3 unpicks what this looks like in practice, with key points and questions to consider for ensuring that all children are making progress in your lessons.

Table 6.3 Key points and questions to consider to support pupil progress

Progress in relation to learning objectives and success criteria
What can I do?
<ul><li>Ensure that learning objectives and associated success criteria are *clear* and targeted according to curriculum attainment targets and ongoing assessment or 'gaps analysis'.</li><li>Consider the *needs* of all children and ensure that the objectives and related tasks are differentiated appropriately. Ensure that resources are appropriate and that any additional adults are used effectively.</li><li>Evaluate each lesson; in particular, consider the impact of your teaching on children's learning. This is a fundamental part of the planning, teaching and assessment cycle; lesson evaluations demonstrate reflection and will help you understand and develop your practice (Warwick and Wolpert, 2018). Ensure that planning is clearly annotated or that notes are made to reflect this.</li><li>Consider how you can ensure children have *ownership* over their learning. Ensure that you evaluate how well children understand the learning objective and consider the techniques to support them in engaging with criteria and self-assessing their learning. For example, when writing, *Children need to learn that it is not just the role of the teacher to read and comment on writing. They need to learn how to evaluate their own and others' writing – how to identify the value in it* (Bearne and Reedy, 2018, p369).</li></ul>
Further questions to consider
<ul><li>Have all children achieved their objective within a session? Have any questions or misconceptions been addressed?</li><li>How effectively were objectives differentiated? Did you make effective provision for those with additional needs?</li></ul>

(Continued)

Table 6.3 (Continued)

• What do they know or are they able to do now that they didn't or couldn't at the start of the session? How do you know? • Have you used formative assessment strategies such as questioning effectively? • How were additional adults used to ensure that all children were making good progress?

Progress in relation to marking and feedback

What can I do?

- Ensure that *formative assessment strategies* are used effectively to inform teaching. For more information on formative assessment, refer to Chapters 3 and 4.
- Consider the impact and effectiveness on your *feedback* and in particular consider the children's response. Remember that effective feedback occurs when it is received and acted upon (Hattie and Clark, 2019), so ensure that children have time to engage with and respond to feedback.

Further questions to consider

- Have you used formative assessment/Assessment for Learning effectively in the session?
- How is this information captured?
- How will any misconceptions be addressed?
- Do children have the opportunity to respond to marking/feedback? How could you facilitate this in lower KS1 or the EYFS?
- How does this inform future planning and teaching?
- Who are you marking for and why?

Progress in relation to target setting and gaps analysis

What can I do?

- Ensure that *targets* are specific, clear and attainable. These should be informed by your ongoing assessment and related to curriculum attainment targets.
- Regularly reflect on children's progress towards targets and consider how you can support children in taking ownership of these. Build in opportunities for *self-assessment* and ensure that children have a clear understanding of what their target is 'asking them to do'.
- Reflect on your practice, adapt your teaching, and plan for interventions and/or guided groups as a result of target setting and ongoing assessment.

Further questions to consider

- Have the children achieved their weekly or termly targets?
- Where is the evidence and how do you know?
- How is this supported by both formative and summative approaches, such as marking and written feedback, end-of-term testing and data tracking?
- What provisions can be put in place for those who have not achieved objectives?
- How can you ensure that interventions are effective?
- How has assessment information and gaps analysis been used to inform this teaching?

Progress in relation to end-of-year/Key Stage expectations
What can I do?
• Plan taught sessions (including units or topics) carefully to ensure for coverage and allow for opportunities to revisit key concepts. Use your ongoing assessment to inform this.
• Ensure that through *ongoing assessment* you have a good picture of the progress of all children throughout the year, and are able to act to close gaps and plan for intervention sessions where necessary.
• Engage with *pupil progress meetings*; use this to support gaps analysis and feed into your planning, teaching and assessment cycle.
• Liaise with the *next class teacher* where possible to ensure that key information is shared and that specific children can be targeted and supported quickly where necessary.
Further questions to consider
• How is this tracked throughout the year?
• What role do pupil progress meetings play?
• What will happen for those pupils who haven't achieved these?

HOW IS PUPIL PROGRESS MEASURED?

In addition to statutory National Curriculum tests and the phonics check at the end of Year 1 in England, schools may use baseline testing to measure progress (at the time of writing, the English government was planning to introduce a statutory Reception baseline assessment in autumn 2020). Schools also commonly use non-statutory end-of-year tests to summatively assess progress in year groups without National Curriculum tests. Often, schools will use online data tracking systems alongside their assessment to monitor pupil progress. This will be further explored in Chapter 7.

Pupil progress can also be measured more formatively within and at the end of taught sessions by using lesson objectives or criteria as a guide. Most teachers will use formative assessment strategies such as questioning and oral or written feedback to reflect on whether pupils have achieved the desired outcome. This may also be recorded on planning documents and added to assessment tracking.

EVIDENCING PUPIL PROGRESS

As explored in Chapter 5, progress in terms of statutory testing is reported to the local authority and government at the end of each Key Stage, with additional information being provided by the Year 1 phonics check. At the end of Key Stage 2 in England, progress is published in the school performance tables. This formal progress measure is based on test outcomes and on prior attainment.

Pupil progress is also monitored throughout all year groups, with attainment often tracked as children move through primary school. Table 6.4 below illustrates a range of sources that you might use to track and record pupil progress. Consider also who might be looking at this evidence and what it means for each of the different stakeholders, as detailed above.

Table 6.4   Evidencing pupil progress

Possible evidence of pupil progress	Specific evidence to consider
Children's work	Meeting, exceeding or working towards learning objective(s).
	Evidence of skills and objectives being embedded, such as within cross-curricular writing.
Marking and feedback	Children's responses to written feedback, including 'next steps' where children might review their work or address misconceptions.
	Self- and peer assessment, including success criteria.
Conversations with children	Pupil conferencing
	Questioning and oral feedback
Assessment tasks	Testing and further examples of formative and summative assessment, such as 'hot and cold tasks', 'big writes' and hinge questions.
Gaps analysis	Specific gaps in knowledge and the steps taken to close these.
	Intervention and small group work planned as a result.
	Different attainment groupings within the class.
Additional forms of evidence	Learning journals/portfolios, etc.
	Floorbooks (see Case study 6.1)
	Teacher assessment/moderation
	Individual progress/targets set
	EHCP/IEP objectives
	Class data tracking

As explored in Table 6.4, evidence of pupil progress can come from a range of different sources and does not need to rely on summative assessment. This is particularly true for foundation subjects where a range of approaches may be used. In Case study 6.1, Penny Hay shares insights into how sketchbooks can be used to support pupil progress in art and design.

CASE STUDY 6.1 ART: CHALLENGING THE NOTION OF LINEAR PROGRESSION – AN EXAMPLE OF USING SKETCHBOOKS IN ART AND DESIGN

Penny Hay, Senior Lecturer in Arts Education, Bath Spa University and Director of Research, 5×5×5=creativity

Art has traditionally has been measured by a sense of progression from less sophisticated to more skilful art production. However, art education in a contemporary context is centred on creative and critical thinking, reflection and the transformative power of art. Mere lists of visual elements, media or domains are insufficient to reflect the complexity of learning in art and design.

Figure 6.2   Child sharing sketchbook (Image courtesy of 5×5×5=creativity)

The notion of linear progression is misleading, especially in relation to art making, as the creative process itself highlights the value of exploration and unexpected outcomes. Giving children the time and freedom to explore ideas without judgement of failure can open up spaces of possibility for them that would otherwise have been closed down by outcome-led approaches to teaching and learning. Self-expression and creativity can be finely balanced with an unfolding repertoire of skills, concepts and knowledge in relation to art and design as a discipline.

The term 'sketchbook' is a misnomer in that it is not merely a book of sketches. Children's visual journals or sketchbooks provide a vehicle for collecting ideas and experiences in a visual form, whether in the form of drawing, sketches, painting, collage, photography, mixed media or secondary source material. These are a valuable personal resource for the development of the children's art making. The visual journal or sketchbook also becomes an artwork in itself, as a personalised book that reflects their individual personality.

Sketchbooks are important for children to develop and record ideas, review and reflect on their work, and maintain a dialogue about their ongoing themes and fascinations. Giving the children the opportunity to annotate their work is an important aspect of developing an ongoing dialogue with them and gives the teacher insight into their ideas. Sketchbooks can create a shared point for conversation about the children's art making and offer a diagnostic tool for the teacher to support the child's individual learning pathway. They help to make the learning visible and act as an integral tool for both the expression of ideas and for meaning-making.

Using sketchbooks opens up a dialogue about children's future explorations and artwork, and provides a point of reference to share ideas. Children can take great pride in keeping their sketchbooks and may share these with peers, teachers, parents and carers (Figures 6.2 and 6.3). Sketchbooks and ongoing artwork can be displayed as documentation of processes rather than solely as the end products.

> *Through observing children engaged in processes of making art, I have seen the children in a different light, I have noticed their own interests and self-chosen themes, and how they have used their imagination to explore ideas.*
>
> (Year 4 teacher, St Andrew's Primary School, Bath)

(Continued)

(Continued)

Giving time for the children to develop their thoughts and ideas through using their sketchbooks to reflect on and process their experiences, children are encouraged to express their thoughts and feelings. Giving children the freedom to follow their own lines of enquiry, supported and scaffolded appropriately, increases motivation, engagement and personal achievement.

Its good because you can look back and see what you've done. Its also nice to see other people's ideas, it made me think about different kinds of art too.

(Year 5 child, Batheaston Primary School)

Figure 6.3   *Children reviewing their work together (Image courtesy of 5×5×5=creativity)*

Ideally, assessments are made by, with and alongside the child. Focus can be given to individual and collaborative work in a range of media and how children use their books to review ideas, making connections with the work of other artists. Assessment can be purposeful if it draws on the observation of children initiating their own learning with adults supporting the child in developing their artwork with sustained interest and enquiry. Subtle and strategic use of assessment, focused on individual children's developing confidence and competence in art and design is vital.

PROGRESSION FOR PUPILS WITH SPECIAL EDUCATIONAL NEEDS OR DISABILITIES

It is important to consider the impact that special educational needs and disabilities (SEND) may have on pupil progress. For children with SEND, age or year-group expectations may not be appropriate. As a teacher, you have a responsibility to ensure that you make provision for all children and, as stated in the Teachers' Standards, *have a clear understanding of the needs of all pupils, including those with special educational needs* (DfE, 2011). You must also ensure that pupils with SEND continue to make good progress.

According to the SEN Code of Practice, class and subject teachers, supported by the senior leadership team, should make regular assessments of progress for all pupils. These should seek to identify pupils making less than expected progress given their age and individual circumstances (DfE and DHSC, 2015).

As Wedell states:

> *The emphasis on assessing pupils' progress, rather than just on the levels of attainment they reach, is obviously very relevant for the evaluation of pupils with SEND, but it also leads to the question whether one can assume that pupils with SEND will progress at an 'age appropriate' rate in all cases.*

> (Wedell, 2017, p359)

The SEN *Code of Practice* continues to state that, in the case of pupils with SEND, this expected progress *can include progress in areas other than attainment – for instance where a pupil needs to make additional progress with wider development or social needs in order to make a successful transition to adult life* (DfE and DHSC, 2015). It is also important to remember that lack of progress and low attainment do not necessarily mean that a child has SEND; however, they may be an indicator of a range of learning difficulties or disabilities. Equally, it should not be assumed that attainment in line with chronological age means that there is no learning difficulty or disability (DfE and DHSC, 2015).

In Case study 6.2, one Special Educational Needs Coordinator (SENCO) describes practice in their school, where teachers may individualise teaching and assessments, as appropriate for the children.

CASE STUDY 6.2 WHAT PROGRESS MIGHT LOOK LIKE FOR CHILDREN WITH SPECIAL EDUCATIONAL NEEDS

Rachel Vaughan, SENCO at Stanbridge Primary School, a large school in South Gloucestershire, explains how pupil progress is monitored and assessed for children with additional needs

Stanbridge Primary School aims for all children to make at least good progress and attainment in all areas of their learning. This is no less the case for children who present with special education needs and disabilities (SEND). Teachers and leaders are confident in adapting planning and teaching in order to meet the needs of SEND children and, in turn, have an individualised approach to assessing their progress.

Stanbridge provides an inclusive learning environment for all children. Children who are identified as having SEND, and are listed on the school SEND register, may complete baseline summative assessments using the National Foundation for Educational Research (NFER) test or, if appropriate, the end of Key Stage Standard Assessment Tests (SATS). The assessments are chosen by the teacher to be in line with their individual attainment expectations and teachers are confident in discretely adapting these where necessary. It is a succinct way of ensuring that SEND children continue to receive provision and challenge appropriate to their learning needs, and identifies their individual development areas. SEND pupils' progress is tracked through termly summative assessments, pupil progress meetings and Individual Education Plans. In order to ensure that they are meeting the needs of SEND children, teachers use the assessment processes to inform SEND children's IEP targets and work collaboratively with pupils and parents to decide on how these will be met. Religious practice of the 'assess, plan, do and review' process ensures that IEP targets are appropriate, challenging and individual.

AN EXAMPLE OF TRACKING PROGRESSION IN THE EARLY YEARS

The structure and expectations for assessment in the Early Years Foundation Stage were introduced in Chapter 5. Here, the focus is on how pupil progression can be recorded with younger children. In Case study 6.3, Reception and Nursery class teachers at a Cheshire primary school use floorbooks as part of their recording and assessment process, usually completing one floorbook per half term. Each floorbook begins with a question that either stems from the children's interests or follows a theme. In Case study 6.2, one Reception teacher gives an overview of how the school uses floorbooks to support and monitor pupil progress.

CASE STUDY 6.3 USING FLOORBOOKS IN THE EARLY YEARS

We always start the year with a floorbook, which is all about the children in the class to help them get to know each other, and to help us (the teaching staff) to get to know the children, their interests and what they could do. This forms part of our informal baseline assessment processes. As the year progresses, the themes for the floorbooks stem from the children themselves - e.g. several children were interested in dinosaurs, so we asked, 'Where have all the dinosaurs gone?' The first question in the floorbook is repeated at the end of the half term and progression can clearly be seen in the responses that the children make.

One recent floorbook that really stands out was all about space and aliens. As several children had expressed an interest in space, we sent a letter to the class from an alien who wanted to find out about us. His letter asked us how we travel on Earth. Our floorbook began by posing this question. The children were able to talk about ways in which they can travel using their bodies (rolling, jumping, etc.) as well as transport. This helped us to ascertain their prior knowledge and any misconceptions they might have. We then recorded our explorations and work relating to travel and space

Figure 6.4 A child in Reception annotates a floorbook

in the floorbook, and asked the same question at the end of the six weeks. The amount that the children had grown in knowledge was astounding. They had even explored gravity and the effects of gravity, and found out about a female astronaut, watching some videos about her life on the International Space Station. The floorbook was a really useful assessment tool and has been used to share information with moderators, Ofsted, local authority advisers, as well as the senior management team in school.

The most exciting thing about using floorbooks is the way that children interact with them (Figure 6.4). They contribute to the floorbook in terms of the initial ideas for themes; we record what they say in verbatim comments, add photographs and pieces of work. Sometimes the children have to decide what to stick in the book and give reasons why each piece is important. They have a great sense of ownership for the books, which remain in the book corner for the year and are often read at storytime. These books have done wonders for children's self-esteem and particularly helped children with more barriers to learning like those with English as an additional language (EAL) to feel valued. In addition, the books are always accessible for parents to see and are a fantastic window into their children's day. Children regularly continue their learning at home, finding out more things relating to our floorbook theme, and we always value this contribution and include this in the book too.

CONCLUSION

In this chapter, we have considered what we mean by pupil progress in practice. This was defined as the developments that children are making towards learning objectives from a given starting point. – i.e. the elements (or stepping stones) required to reach and achieve an attainment target. This chapter focused on ways to promote and evidence pupil progress, exploring examples from different subjects and phases. The chapter started to introduce pupil progress meetings and associated whole-school data tracking and analysis, which will be further explored in the next chapter.

As a class teacher, you have a responsibility to ensure that all children make good progress. Considering the children's starting point and their levels of achievement can help to enable this and help you to identify any gaps in progress. It is also important to remember that progress is not linear and will fluctuate depending on many factors. If you have concerns about pupil progress, including the progress of specific children, you should discuss this with your colleagues; depending on the size and structure of your school, this might include the SENCO, school assessment or data lead, Key Stage leader, deputy or headteacher.

REFERENCES

Assessment Reform Group (ARG) (2002) *Assessment for Learning: 10 Principles: Research-based Principles to Guide Classroom Practice*. Cambridge: University of Cambridge School of Education.

Bearne, E and Reedy, D (2018) *Teaching Primary English: Subject Knowledge and Classroom Practice*. Abingdon: Routledge.

Department for Education (DfE) (2011) *Teachers' Standards*. London: DfE.

Department for Education (DfE) (2013) *National Curriculum in England*. London: DfE.

Department for Education (DfE) (2018) Press release: Chief Inspector sets out vision for new Education Inspection Framework. Available online at: www.gov.uk/government/news/chief-inspector-sets-out-vision-for-new-education-inspection-framework

Department for Education and Department of Health and Social Care (DfE and DHSC) (2015) *Special Educational Needs and Disability Code of Practice: 0 to 25 years*. London: DfE.

General Teaching Council for Northern Ireland (GTCNI) (2011) *Teaching: The Reflective Profession*. Belfast: GTCNI.

General Teaching Council (GTC) for Scotland (2012) *The Standards for Registration: Mandatory Requirements for Registration with the General Teaching Council for Scotland*. Edinburgh: GTC Scotland.

Harford, S (2018) Ofsted blog: Schools, early years, further education and skills. April. Assessment – what are inspectors looking at? Available online at: https://educationinspection.blog.gov.uk/2018/04/23/assessment-what-are-inspectors-looking-at/

Hattie, J and Clarke, S (2019) *Visible Learning: Feedback*. Abingdon: Routledge.

Ofsted (2018) *School inspection handbook*. Manchester: Ofsted.

Warwick, J and Wolpert, A (2018) Making the most of your placements. In Cremin, T and Burnett, C, *Learning to Teach in the Primary School* (4th edn). Abingdon: Routledge, pp32–47.

Wedell, K (2017) Points from the SENCo Forum: reporting pupil progress. *British Journal of Special Education*, 44(3): 359–61.

Welsh Government (2017) *Professional Standards for Teaching and Leadership*. Cardiff: Welsh Government.

7
USING DATA TO SUPPORT SCHOOL IMPROVEMENT

DARREN MCKAY

PURPOSE OF THIS CHAPTER

In this chapter we will:

- examine how data can be used to support your teaching and children's learning;

- develop an understanding of the way data is used to measure pupil progress and hold you to account;

- explore how data may be used by key stakeholders including teachers, senior leaders and external agencies.

INTRODUCTION

Data is the driving force for school improvement. In Wales, for example, Challenge Advisers were established in 2014 with a clear directive to *take a data driven approach to supporting and challenging the leadership in schools to improve* (EAS of South East Wales, 2017). School Improvement Partners (SIPs) in England had the same data-led approach.

For decades, primary schools have generated a wealth of data based on children's outcomes. As a deputy headteacher, I remember collating data from classes and spending hours inputting it into vast spreadsheets covering the whole school. This was then interrogated to create commentaries, tables, charts and graphs to share with teachers, senior leaders, governors, school improvement partners and the Office for Standards in Education (Ofsted) inspectors. At specified times in a child's schooling, the data was also shared with the local authority (LA) and the government to fulfil statutory requirements. Children's educational development was captured as a series of letters and numbers, and converted into points of progress. In this chapter, we will discuss how data is and can be used, and the importance of remembering that there is a living, breathing child behind every number who experiences the highs and lows of life in the twenty-first century.

This chapter begins by briefly reviewing how and why school leaders have become 'number crunchers' and can appear to be preoccupied with data. The chapter will then define some key terms within a primary school context and explore why data is more than a collection of numbers. Case studies will be used to illustrate how two schools have successfully used data to support school improvement and still keep the child at the centre of their analysis. Finally, the chapter will consider the current relationship between Ofsted and data produced at a school level.

WHY HAS DATA BECOME KING?

My relationship with data has developed over the years. When I was a newly qualified teacher (NQT) in the mid 1990s, teaching a Year 5 class, the data I collected was for my own use and was kept in my mark book. It consisted of scores the children gained in multiplication and spelling tests – i.e. a number indicating how many each child got right; a tick if homework had been handed in; who had been heard reading by the volunteer and other information I deemed useful. It was my record of the information I felt was important. The only other person who looked at the mark book was a teaching assistant (TA) who worked with a child for three hours a week. My mark book was not shared with senior leaders or other colleagues. I shared the information at parent consultation meetings to add some context to our discussion, but kept the contents of my book to myself the rest of the time. How useful this data was to the parents is debatable, but both parties in the meeting seemed to feel these numbers were of importance. In 1997, my relationship with data started to develop and mature. I was asked to complete a new set of tests with my Year 4 class. These were the reading, writing and maths optional standard attainment tests, widely known as optional SATs, produced by the Qualifications and Curriculum Authority (QCA), a UK non-department public body sponsored by the Department of Education and Skills (DfES) (Massey at al., 2002). These tests were primarily designed to help prepare children for the Year 6 statutory assessments. Suddenly, data had become more important to me as a class teacher. I was asked to use the raw scores to calculate age-standardised results (scaled scores) and record these on a sheet to be shared with the senior leadership team. Data was no longer the marks in my book, but had become something else that the senior leaders could use to hold me to account.

Accountability is a well-established aspect of what it means to be a primary school teacher today, and it has become common practice to use data as a criterion of accountability. McKay (2019) explored this relationship in more depth and discussed how this accountability changes as a teacher's career develops. My personal experience of this specific type of accountability started with the introduction of the optional tests mentioned above. I started to hear colleagues talk about the percentage of children who had achieved the 'magic number' of correct answers in their test, indicating they could be judged to be at an acceptable level. This shift to talking about children as numbers was not new to teachers of Year 2 and Year 6. These colleagues had been using this language for several years. However, in the rest of the primary phase, we talked about children using non-numerical nomenclature; we thought and talked about them using their names. With the introduction of these high-stakes tests, there was a risk of children being reduced to a set of numbers. Data was becoming king.

A culture of numerical target setting, led by the outcomes of statutory testing in Year 6, had been present since the introduction of the Year 2 and Year 6 statutory tasks and tests between 1991 and 1995.

These assessments were produced in direct response to the UK government's introduction of the National Curriculum (NC) for England and Wales, as defined in Part 1 of the Act (Education Reform Act, 1988). Table 7.1 gives a summary of the changes to the curriculum in England since this Act and helps to illustrate how data has become the driving force for school improvement.

Table 7.1 An overview of the changes to the National Curriculum for England: 1988–2015

Date	Directive	Impact on assessment
1988	Education Reform Act introduces the National Curriculum (NC) in England and Wales. In primary schools, there were three core subjects (English, mathematics and science; with Welsh as the fourth in Welsh-speaking schools) and six foundation subjects (history, geography, technology, music, art and physical education).	Criterion-referenced summative assessment at the end of each Key Stage (Year 2 and Year 6) in relation to the first six attainment targets: levels 1 to 6: • KS1 covers levels 1-3 • KS2 covers levels 2-6
1991-5	Statutory Tasks and Tests introduced, initially in Year 2 and then Year 6.	Tasks to assess reading, writing, mathematics and science at the end of Year 2 were reviewed and tests were introduced for reading and mathematics. Year 6 statutory tests were introduced for reading, writing, mathematics and science. Teacher assessment using the attainment targets for each subject of the NC was made.
1994	The NC and its Assessment: Final Report (Dearing Review) calls for a slimmed-down primary NC; one was introduced in 1995.	Criterion-referenced summative assessment at the end of each Key Stage (Year 2 and Year 6) in relation to the first six attainment targets: levels 1-6. Attainment at end of Key Stage: • KS1 levels 1-3 • KS2 levels 3-5 Schools quickly adopted the mantra Year 2, level 2; Year 6, level 4.
1998	Foundation subjects are disapplied to allow a focus on literacy and numeracy. The Literacy and Numeracy Strategies were introduced.	Teachers are not only told what to teach, but also how to teach it. Assessment requirements are unchanged.
1999	New NC in England introduced in 2000; focus on English, mathematics and science. Reduced content for foundation subjects. Wales devises own curriculum.	KS1 and KS2 attainment targets for levels 1-6 revised to meet new curriculum.

(Continued)

Table 7.1   (Continued)

Date	Directive	Impact on assessment
2005	Tests in Year 2 downgraded and although still statutory, the requirement is that they inform summative teacher assessment (TA).	Tests in KS1 used to support TA.
2008	The Independent Review of the Primary Curriculum: Final Report (Rose Review) led to proposed changes to the NC, removing ten subjects and introducing six areas of learning, implementation in schools due in September 2010. Change of UK government in May 2010 stopped this.	2000 National Curriculum remained statutory.
2010	Science SAT abolished for KS2.	TA of science only at end of KS2.
2014	New subject-focused NC.	New testing arrangements introduced in 2016. Scaled scores to replace levels. Levels replaced in: • Years 1, 3, 4, 5 in 2014/15. • Years 2 and 6 in 2015 for 2016 SATs.
2015	Final report of the Commission on Assessment without levels published (McIntosh Report).	Schools directed to design own summative assessment process. Most schools adopted a criterion-referenced summative assessment or levels by a different name.

WHY IS DATA MORE THAN A SET OF NUMBERS?

There is a danger when analysing data that we forget that the purpose for the analysis is to confirm what teachers and children do well so they can continue doing it, what they need to stop doing because it does not work, and what they could do instead. As long as we remember that the data is centred in the children's learning and is only part of what defines each child, we should be able to use data to transform children's lives. I am a self-confessed number cruncher, yet I whole-heartedly believe that the story behind the data is far more valuable and interesting than the collection of numbers the data is often reduced to.

KEY DEFINITIONS

There are some key terms that are used in schools when discussing and analysing data. It is important that the parties involved in these discussions are in agreement about what each term means within the context of teaching and learning. For the purposes of this chapter, the following six words need a clear definition within the context of school data.

- Data

- Tracking

- Accountability

- Attainment

- Progress

- Impact

It is useful to note that none of these terms are synonymous with assessment. For example, tracking software that aggregates scores to provide a result is not providing an assessment of the child. The tracker does not make a judgement; it may provide useful information, but the teacher must decide how to use that information to support the children's learning. Software packages can provide useful ways of collating and storing data, mirroring an electronic mark book or portfolio. The aim of this chapter is not to review the rapidly changing marketplace, but to provide the teacher with the understanding to be able to judge what purpose they would like the software to fulfil.

Table 7.2 gives an appropriate dictionary definition and then an explanation of what each means within the context of a primary school.

Table 7.2   Definitions of key terms used in school data analysis

Key term	An appropriate dictionary definition	What this means within the context of school data
Data	Facts and statistics collected together for reference or analysis	The information collected about each child's learning. This is most commonly translated into a letter or number to identify the child's attainment against a set of criteria. These criteria are closely linked to the curriculum provision and usually linked to EYFS Development Matters and Early Learning Goals (ELGs) and NC age-related expectations (AREs).
Tracking	To note the progress or course of	There is an expectation from the government that a child should be able to apply the skills and demonstrate the attitudes, dispositions and knowledge set out in the NC AREs. It would seem logical, therefore, for teachers to know if the children they teach are likely to meet, exceed or fall short of those AREs. Children's attainment and progress are monitored and judgements are made about the trajectory of each child's learning towards attaining these AREs. If the child may not reach the ARE, additional learning experiences may need to be given.

(Continued)

Table 7.2 (Continued)

Key term	An appropriate dictionary definition	What this means within the context of school data
Accountability	To be accountable (required or expected to justify actions or decisions; responsible)	Teachers are held to account for the outcomes of each child by the stakeholders in that child's learning. These are the child, parents, school leaders, governing bodies, multi-academy trusts, local authority, Ofsted and the teacher herself.
Attainment	A thing achieved, especially a skill or educational achievement	A judgement of what the child can do in relation to the set criteria. This could be in the form of a description, grade, level, number, verb or letter. Attainment can be against statutory benchmarks or those set by the teacher or school leaders.
Progress	Development towards an improved or more advanced condition	A measure of the improvement, or not, made by a child from a given starting point. Progress can be expressed as a number or adjective. At KS2, statutory progress is no longer reported for individual children. However, a school's progress score for reading, writing and maths is reported (see section below on Ofsted for further explanation).

WHY DO SCHOOLS TRACK PUPIL PROGRESS?

The short answer is accountability. One way in which teachers are held to account is by tracking pupils' progress. If a child is not, or group of children are not, making the expected progress set by either the school leaders, multi-academy trust (MAT) or government, the sooner this is identified, the sooner intervention can be started to support the individuals to develop. It is also beneficial to identify those individuals who are exceeding the expected progress, to identify possible reasons, and to see if strategies can be replicated and/or adapted to support others. In this sense, data is being used in a formative way to support pupil progress. Harlen (2012) suggests that there needs to be caution when attempting to use data in a truly formative way and warns that summative assessment based on tests cannot be used in a truly formative way, but can help to identify further learning. I would argue that this use of summative assessment data is a worthwhile activity as long as we do not overestimate the impact it can have on children's learning and the task is not too onerous on the teacher completing the analysis.

A well-established way to help teachers to remember that data is more than a set of numbers is the practice known as Pupil Progress Reviews (PPR). A PPR usually consists of a meeting between a class teacher and a senior leader in which they discuss the progress and attainment of children in the class. To do this in detail for each child would take too long, so often particular groups provide a focus; alternatively, the teacher may select pupils who they feel are under-performing. Discussions may include comparison of pupil assessment data or work samples over time. The aim by the end of the meeting is to have agreed strategies or interventions that will be put in place to support the individuals or groups who have been identified in need of additional support or an alternative approach. Case study 7.1 describes a different approach to PPR, where the teaching team also meet as a larger group.

CASE STUDY 7.1 A FORMER HEADTEACHER OF A PRIMARY SCHOOL IN ENGLAND, LYNN SALTER, DESCRIBES THE PROCESS OF THE PUPIL PROGRESS REVIEW

Whole-school strategic objectives were agreed annually in the school development plan and headteacher's performance management. Pupil Progress Reviews (PPRs) were a key vehicle for the staff to work together to close identified performance gaps and to maximise achievement for all children.

Summative assessment data from the school's tracking system was used to support teachers and senior leaders to analyse children's performance, taking into account their Early Years Foundation Stage (EYFS) baseline, their current level of attainment and their progress towards end of Key Stage targets. Different pupil groupings were compared – e.g. the achievement of boys vs. girls; service pupils vs. non-service (Armed Forces families); and the achievement of significant groups was reviewed – e.g. EAL, SEND, pupil premium and high attainers.

During the year, PPR meetings took place termly and formed an integral part of both the performance appraisal and school's monitoring and evaluation processes. The meetings took two distinct forms.

- One-to-one PPR meetings between individual teachers and their line managers, as part of their annual performance management cycle.

- Phase team progress review meetings between all the year group teachers, the Key Stage lead, headteacher, deputy headteacher and SENCO.

During the one-to-one meetings, individual targets were set that linked to the overall school development objectives. The final meeting was held once end-of-year assessments and statutory assessment results were known, so that overall annual performance could be reviewed.

The phase team progress review meetings proved to be powerful opportunities to discuss and share what was working well for individual children, groups or classes, and to cascade this success across the phase team by pooling resources and targeting interventions (including TA and specific SEN support). During these meetings, teachers and senior leaders also moderated outcomes in pupils' books across the classes, ensuring that the summative assessment data reflected parity in outcomes. Most importantly, staff collaborated to craft solutions to accelerate learning.

The cycle of meetings was designed to support and challenge each member of the school community to achieve the best outcomes for the children. This led to a sense of individual accountability for pupil progress, underpinned by team support and challenge, firmly embedded in the school development plan.

(Continued)

(Continued)

This case study illustrates how teachers and senior leaders can achieve a data-led, whole-school approach to school improvement. By participating in PPR meetings two or possibly three times a year, teachers can take time away from the classroom and focus on what the children they teach *can do* and what can be implemented to help those children *progress*.

DATA ANALYSIS AT DIFFERENT LEVELS

Figure 7.1 illustrates the key levels of data analysis from the individual child to comparisons with national data. As you can see, at each level the question to ask is something akin with, 'How are we doing compared with . . . ?'. So when judging the attainment (shown in italics) of the individual child, you need to compare them with the age-related expectation (ARE) to give an indication of their attainment. However, you must also factor in the child's starting point, any additional needs such as SEN, (including long-term or short-term social or emotional needs), EAL, or if the child is new to the school. This does not mean that your expectations should be lowered but that it should be centred in the needs of the child by taking their context into account. Again, we come back to the essential story behind the data. The same context needs to be applied to the judgement made about the child's progress.

Child	Class	Key Stage	School	National
ARE: developing towards, mastering or at greater depth	*Number and % ARE: developing towards, mastering or at greater depth*	*Number and % ARE: developing towards, mastering or at greater depth*	*Number and % ARE: developing towards, mastering or at greater depth*	*Compare school with National number and % ARE: developing towards, mastering or at greater depth*
Progress: below expected, expected or exceeding expected	Progress: number and % below expected, expected or exceeding expected	Progress: number and % below expected, expected or exceeding expected	Progress: number and % below expected, expected or exceeding expected	Compare school with National progress score

Figure 7.1   Comparisons to be made at each level of data analysis

There are questions to be asked at each level of data analysis. Figure 7.2 below helps to guide you through the analysis by identifying key questions that could be asked. This is by no means an exhaustive list, but more of an illustration of the process. The initial question regards reliability, asks whether the data can be trusted for comparison. This should be considered at a level appropriate for the age, stage and purpose of assessment. For example, if the data under discussion is pupil writing, then it is appropriate to consider the level of independence in the work for comparison between pupils or over time. However, if the data is maths test scores, it may be important for comparisons to be made based on the same or similar tests.

Analysis of data, whether it is by individual class teachers, groups of teachers or senior leaders, leads to the drawing of conclusions. As identified in Figure 7.2, such conclusions should lead to actions, examples of which are provided in Table 7.3.

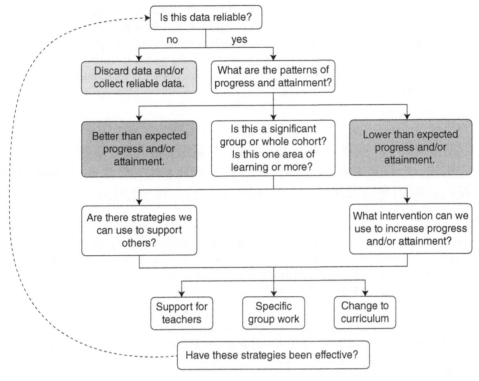

Figure 7.2   Key questions for data analysis

Table 7.3   Possible actions resulting from data analysis

Possible actions	Examples of actions
Support for teachers	Observe colleague teaching similar topic, discuss strategies for support with teacher in the year below, or extension strategies with teacher in the year above, support with planning to break down outcome into smaller steps, exploration of exemplification materials.
Specific group work	Additional input for identified group, change of groupings, different set of strategies utilised, different focus for group work, extended focus on particular element.
Change to curriculum	More time allocated to focus on particular element, lessons/topics reordered, year group or school subject day planned to focus on one element, cyclical sessions planned to allow return to reinforce previously covered topics.

Case study 7.2 explores how data is used at each level of teaching and learning to support school improvement. The class teachers, senior managers and governors analyse the data to identify strengths and areas to improve. Data is collected and analysed to guide curriculum planning, hold staff to account and justify choices made by the school leadership team. The Challenge Adviser, an external adviser to the school appointed by the regional school improvement consortia working on behalf of the LA, uses the school's statutory and internal data to ensure that *schools are equipped to drive and sustain improvements in raising standards and providing high quality educational provision* (Welsh Government, 2014, p2). The intricacy of how to create a fair comparison between schools with different contexts is addressed when the headteacher explains why the data of a specific group of children is analysed as a distinct cohort, separate from the whole-school data, again illustrating that understanding the story behind the data is essential and fascinating.

CASE STUDY 7.2 BETHAN PETERSON, HEADTEACHER OF WHITESTONE PRIMARY SCHOOL, SWANSEA, EXPLAINS HOW DATA ANALYSIS IS A KEY ELEMENT OF SCHOOL SELF-EVALUATION AND IMPROVEMENT

Data is used in a variety of ways at Whitestone Primary School as a valuable tool in the self-evaluation processes and monitoring of pupil progress, with the goal of ensuring that all pupils realise their fullest potential and to eliminate underachievement. The school's ethos is based on the belief that every pupil is an individual, and our aim is to ensure that learning and teaching meets the needs of pupils at a level appropriate to them. Assessment data, both formal and informal, is therefore essential in understanding the needs of each pupil.

Teacher Assessment data is used to track and monitor pupil achievement across the school from Nursery through to Year 6. Where pupils are identified as underperforming, the learning opportunities offered are critiqued and appropriate strategies are implemented. Differentiation is a key strength of our school and necessary to ensure the high levels of inclusion offered. This differentiation of the curriculum is not possible without the forensic examination of school data, including question-level analysis of National Test data where staff 'drill down' to analyse the performance of key pupil groups such as 'ever Free School Meals' (eFSM), gender and Additional Learning Needs (ALN). This analysis leads to a bespoke curriculum delivery and school improvement through the raising of standards. Pupil data is used to support the evaluation of the effectiveness of the strategy by teaching staff and school governors.

Data is used in a variety of ways to directly support school improvement and to evaluate the effectiveness of our provision. These include the following:

- Staff Performance Management is evidenced by pupil data.

- Governors monitor school improvement by interrogating the pupil attainment and achievement data, identifying strengths and areas for development.

- Subject and Aspect Leaders monitor pupil progress at sub-level to identify trends, strengths and areas for development within their area of responsibility.

- Meetings with the Challenge Adviser, to hold the school management team to account for school processes and improvement.

- Targets set at all levels are monitored and measured against pupil achievement.

Whitestone Primary School has two Specialist Teaching Facilities for pupils with moderate to severe learning difficulties. Due to the nature of the needs of these pupils, their baseline/on-entry assessment scores are generally lower than their peers in the mainstream classes. As a result, it is appropriate to disaggregate this data set from the whole-school data so that a fair comparison can be made between our school and others across the local authority. As a result of the unique make-up of our school community, staff at all levels at Whitestone consider the progress of pupils at our school alongside their attainment. 'Value added' is an important tool in assessing the progress of the individual pupil; the smallest of steps can and should be celebrated.

HOW OFSTED USES SCHOOL DATA

The Office for Standards in Education, Children's Services and Skills (Ofsted) is a non-ministerial department of the English government. It uses data generated by statutory assessments and recorded on the school census as one of the main criteria to decide if a school needs an inspection. Once an inspection has been triggered, data informs their lines of enquiry. Each year, Ofsted produces Inspection Data Summary Reports (IDSR) that compare a school's statutory assessment data with national data. It also compares the data of significant groups. These consider children:

- who have been in receipt of free school meals at any point in the previous six years: Ever 6 FSM;

- with English as an additional language: EAL;

- with identified special educational needs: SEN;

- who are looked after by the LA: CLA;

- by gender.

The data reported includes the percentage and number of children at the end of Year 2 and Year 6 who attain the expected or better as one group, and those who attained greater depth as a second group, for reading, writing and maths. Science attainment is reported as those who attained the expected standard. Foundation Stage Profile results and Year 1 phonics testing are also included. For each of the data sets, all children in the school's cohort and those identified as disadvantaged are compared with the national performance. Progress measures are also included. These are based on the aggregated results for the cohort when compared with the progress of all children with a similar context and starting point. A progress score of zero indicates that a school's progress is in line with that of similar children nationally. A positive score indicates better progress and a negative score indicates less progress. These reports are available to schools electronically via a password-protected portal.

Another accountability measure used by the DfE and Ofsted is the government definition for floor standard (low scoring) and for coasting standard (low progress). These are used to identify schools not judged by Ofsted to be inadequate, but that may still require support. The standards are measured using statutory assessment data. The support offered by the DfE is in the form of *free advice and support from a national leader of education* (DfE, 2018) and may include additional funding ring-fenced for school improvement.

This heavy reliance on data by the DfE and Ofsted to make judgements regarding the standard of education offered by a school has led many to question what is happening to the curriculum in primary schools. It is not a great leap to conclude that school leaders may feel forced to focus on raising

standards in English and mathematics above all else. It is not being suggested that it is not important to do everything in our power as teachers to help children achieve as highly as they can in
English and mathematics, but the question is whether this should be at the expense of other areas of
the curriculum. Harlen (2014) suggested that we question this climate of data-driven accountability,
as it could lead school leaders to lose sight of a broad and balanced curriculum, instead focusing on
English and mathematics to support children to meet or surpass externally set standards.

Updates to the Ofsted inspection framework appear to respond to such concerns, proposing a greater
focus on the curriculum, together with the proportionate collection of data.

> *The collection of data can also create an additional workload for leaders and staff. Inspectors will look
> at whether schools' collections of attainment or progress data are proportionate and represent an effi-
> cient use of school resources, and are sustainable for staff. The report of the Teacher Workload Advisory
> Group, 'Making data work', recommends that school leaders should not have more than two or three
> data collection points a year, and that these should be used to inform clear actions.*
>
> (Ofsted, 2019, p44)

CONCLUSION

Data-led accountability with league tables of school performance published by the media and statutory
assessment focusing on English and mathematics all exert external pressure on schools, leading many
to give the lion's share of the school's curriculum to English and mathematics. At the time of writing,
there have been suggestions that the focus of school inspection should be broader than the data produced and centre on the curriculum rather than principally on the outcomes of statutory assessment of
English and mathematics (Ofsted, 2019).

This chapter proposes that data is a powerful tool to help us raise standards in primary schools; however, as stated above, the story behind the data must not be ignored and should be understood when
analysing the data of your class. Headteacher Michael Tidd (2018) supported this proposal when he
suggested that we need to know more than the children's names and the data produced about the class
to teach them effectively. The question to ask is, 'What is the impact, on teaching and learning, of the
data produced in your school?'

REFERENCES

Dearing Review (1994) *The National Curriculum and its Assessment: Final Report*. London: School
Curriculum and Assessment Authority.

DfE (2018) *Primary School Accountability in 2018: A Technical Guide for Primary Maintained Schools,
Academies and Free Schools*. Crown copyright.

Education Reform Act 1988, *c. 40*. Available online at: www.legislation.gov.uk/ukpga/1988/40/pdfs/
ukpga_19880040_en.pdf (accessed 11/01/19).

Education Achievement Service (EAS) of South East Wales (2017) *Structure [of the service]*. Available online
at: https://sewales.org.uk/Structure.aspx (accessed 20/01/19).

Harlen, W (2012) On the relationship between assessment for formative and summative purposes. In Gardner, J (ed.) *Assessment and Learning* (2nd edn). London: SAGE, pp. 87–102.

Harlen, W (2014) *Assessment, Standards and Quality of Learning in Primary Education*. York: Cambridge Primary Review Trust.

Massey, A, Green, S, Dexter, T and Hamnett, L (2002) *Comparability of National Tests Over Time: Key Stage Test Standards between 1996 and 2001. Final Report to the QCA of the Comparability Over Time Project.* Available online at: https://core.ac.uk/download/pdf/4156159.pdf (accessed 11/01/19).

McIntosh, J (Chair) (2015) *Final Report of the Commission on Assessment without Levels.* Crown copyright.

McKay, D (2019) Is data the whole story? The data-led accountability of teachers. In Carden, C (ed.) *Primary Teaching: Learning and Teaching in Primary Schools Today.* London: Teaching Matters, pp. 425–41.

Ofsted (2019) *School Inspection Handbook: Draft for Consultation – January 2019.* London: Ofsted.

Rose, J (2009) *Independent Review of the Primary Curriculum: Final Report.* Nottingham: DCSF Publications.

Tidd, M (2018) No one knows a class like their class teacher. TES. Available online at: www.tes.com/news/no-one-knows-class-their-class-teacher (accessed 02/12/18).

Welsh Government (2014) *National Standards for Challenge Advisers.* Crown copyright.

8

MODERATION FOR PROFESSIONAL LEARNING

SARAH EARLE AND TAMSIN GRIMMER

PURPOSE OF THIS CHAPTER

In this chapter we will:

- define and consider the purposes of moderation;

- explore a range of approaches to moderation;

- consider the use of moderation as a way of developing teacher professional learning.

INTRODUCTION

Moderation is the way that we, as a profession, are able to develop an understanding of 'what a good one looks like', or what it looks like not to have 'got there' yet or 'gone further'. Moderation activities can support both reliability of judgements and developing a shared understanding of what progression looks like in a subject. Taking part in moderation can be both challenging and enlightening, but it is essential to understand the purpose of such activities in order to make them useful and meaningful. This chapter does not equate moderation with a 'rubber-stamping' exercise, but considers it to be a process that can enhance professional learning for all involved.

The chapter will begin with a discussion regarding the different meanings and purposes assigned to moderation. There will then be exploration of a range of examples to demonstrate a variety of statutory and non-statutory moderation approaches. The chapter will finish with a discussion regarding ways to use moderation for professional learning.

MODERATION AND STANDARDISATION: DEFINITIONS AND PURPOSES

As with all terminology associated with assessment, 'moderation' can mean different things to different people. For some, 'moderation' is the monitoring of examination answers, for others it is about comparing pupil work to exemplars, while others picture a heated discussion regarding grade boundaries or a dialogue around expected standards. Moderation is a form of checking, with the ultimate aim of agreeing a judgement about an outcome, but it can take many forms, depending on its purpose. Some examples of moderation are briefly described in Table 8.1, in order to show the variety of practice that can be labelled as 'moderation'.

Table 8.1   Examples of the variety of moderation approaches

Example	Purpose of assessment	Purpose of moderation	Common moderation techniques
End-of-school exams	Grading to award a qualification	Ensure consistency in grades	Anonymous/double-blind marking; check application of mark scheme in a sample
Early Years profile	Summarise attainment	Consistency across schools	Within-school comparison, external sampling and verification of standard
Writing teacher assessment	Ascertain attainment in writing	Consistency of standard across schools	Exemplification materials and detailed criteria for within-school comparison; external sampling; 'comparative judgement' (see below)
School self-evaluation	Identify areas of strength and priorities for improvement across school	Provide an external viewpoint	External peer review or school improvement adviser

As can be seen from the table, moderation can vary along a number of dimensions, as summarised below.

- **Outcome to be moderated:** single item or multiple items; from a single occasion or from a period of time.

- **Focus for moderation:** individual pupils, year group or whole school.

- **Criteria for moderation:** mark scheme, curriculum statements, exemplification.

- **Process of moderation:** comparison with criteria, exemplification or other pieces (as in 'comparative judgement' – see section below on writing moderation).

- **Moderator:** individual or group; internal (e.g. across year group) or external peer (e.g. across schools) or by an external agent (e.g. local authority adviser or regional schools commissioner).

If the moderation activity is largely focused on checking consistency in the application of the standards, then 'standardisation' is perhaps a more appropriate term. Standardisation is when children's work is compared to criteria or exemplification materials to enhance inter-rater reliability, whereas moderation includes this, but can also be described more broadly, since it also considers the process of making judgements and the professional dialogue associated with the decision-making. *Standardisation is intended to ensure that individual assessors are applying similar standards, moderation is aimed at groups of assessors working together* (Isaacs et al., 2013, p90). Such group moderation involves working together, discussing both the criteria and the work, to develop an understanding of the expected standard.

Moderation aims to focus on the pupil outcomes, to achieve consistency of judgements, both in the application of criteria (quality control) and the prevention of error and bias (quality assurance) (Harlen, 2007, p76). As teachers, we would like to think that we are free of biases; however, as humans we rely on preconceived ideas about how the world works to be able to get on with our day. We have expectations about where the coffee cups are, what will happen in assembly and how best to mount a display, etc. These preconceived ideas help us to function, but it is also important to be aware that we will have such conceptions about the children in our class. We expect certain pupils to behave and per-form in certain ways, which helps us to tailor our teaching. However, for some this will also mean that we put a ceiling on their attainment, because we will not expect them to be able to access higher levels of work. During assessment and moderation it is important to be aware of these preconceived ideas or biases, so that we are not making judgements in advance. When providing an open-ended activity, some pupils may surprise you: this is a sign that they have not done what you expected them to do – they are challenging your biases. An informal moderation discussion with a colleague regarding some classwork can help to focus on the outcome rather than the individual, looking at what they can do, rather than what you expected them to do.

Moderation is hailed as *potentially the most effective strategy for ensuring both validity and reliability in teacher assessment* (Johnson, 2013, p99), supporting both consistency of judgement and teacher understanding of the breadth of the domain. Nevertheless, concerns regarding reliability of teacher assessment persist: *the accountability function impedes the ability to use assessment as an integral part of the learning process, placing the teacher in a conflicted position* (Green and Oates, 2009, p233). If the assess-ment has 'high stakes' in that it is likely to be used to hold teachers and schools to account, then it is difficult to remain focused on purely the pupil outcome under discussion. For example, when assessing a piece of work which on this occasion falls below the expected standard, it is hard not to take into account all the other pieces of work in which the child had met the criteria, or rephrase the question during the activity to support understanding. However, this is where it is essential to step back and consider the purpose of the assessment. If the purpose is to summarise attainment, then a broader range of evidence can be taken into account. As long as teachers have a good understanding of the assessment criteria, then teacher assessment can provide a valid summary across a range of contexts. However, if the aim of the assessment is to compare pupils across different schools, then some sort of standardisation in assessment conditions is necessary. The conflict arises when an assessment is meant to be a summary judgement for the pupil, but it is also used to compare schools, as for Key Stage 2 in England, there are too many purposes (Stobart, 2009).

For teachers working in a system of high accountability, assessment literacy is essential. Understanding the conflict described above helps to select the most appropriate practice. For example, when decid-ing how much support the pupils should have with a task, the teacher could consider whether the task's primary purpose is for comparison between schools (in which case, it may need more standard instructions); or if the task is a normal piece of classroom work which could inform a later summary (in which case, supporting the child is completely appropriate). Each teaching episode does not need to be treated like a test situation; the teacher can 'step back' to see what the child can do, but also 'step back in' to teach further, responding formatively to the needs of the pupils. Moderation activities that are not 'high stakes', which are for internal monitoring and staff development, can be based on typi-cal classroom activities, since discussion can include the support that different pupils have needed to access the task. Even cross-school moderation can use typical classroom work, if the aim of the moderation discussions are for professional learning, rather than standardisation (see Case study 8.2).

In order to reach agreement about whether pupil outcomes meet the expected standard, practitioners need to develop understanding of the standard or criteria. A *shared conception of achievement* is required for criterion-referenced assessment (Davis, 1998, p139). If there is a *lack of clarity in and applicability of assessment criteria*, the assessment judgement is less reliable (Johnson, 2013, p98). Developing a shared understanding of the criteria also helps support teaching, since such discussions lead on to a clearer view of progression in the subject – what it looks like to get 'better' at it.

EXAMPLES OF APPROACHES TO MODERATION

EARLY YEARS FOUNDATION STAGE PROFILE

As noted in Chapter 5, the Early Years Foundation Stage profile is a statutory assessment in England, which summarises children's attainment at the end of the Early Years Foundation Stage (EYFS), the Reception year when children are aged 4–5. This summative assessment is informed by all the information and observations collated by Reception class teachers throughout the year (see Figure 8.1). Teachers make a judgement about children's progress for every Early Learning Goal in terms of whether they have been met (expected), not yet met (emerging) or go beyond the expected level (exceeding) (as described in Table 5.2). In addition, teachers are asked to provide a written summary describing each child in relation to the *Characteristics of Effective Learning*, as described within the Statutory Framework (DfE, 2017). These characteristics are under three headings: 'Playing and Exploring' (engagement), 'Active Learning' (motivation), and 'Creating and Thinking Critically' (thinking). They look at how children learn rather than what they are learning – for example, considering children's willingness to have a go, ability to concentrate and problem solve (see Table 8.2).

Table 8.2   Example of Characteristics of Effective Learning summary (a short commentary completed by the teacher at the end of EYFS, passed on to parents and Year 1 teachers)

Playing and Exploring - engagement
• Finding out and exploring.   • Playing with what they know.   • Being willing to have a go.
Xavier is a curious boy who enjoys learning by doing. He is happiest when he is learning outside. Xavier usually wants to join in with class activities and particularly enjoys physically active sessions. He has a huge knowledge about animals - in particular, mini-beasts and dinosaurs. Xavier is able to take risks in his learning and engage in new activities. He feels most confident when he is with his friends, Henry and Alex.
Active Learning - motivation
• Being involved and concentrating.   • Keeping trying.   • Enjoying achieving what they set out to do.

(Continued)

Table 8.2 (Continued)

> Xavier is able to maintain attention and concentration for fairly long periods of time when relating to something he is interested in and finds it a little harder to concentrate if the activity is not active. He is fascinated by mini-beasts and can often be found in the outside area looking for creatures. He also regularly collects sticks and stones when outside. He enjoys sharing his findings with the class. He recently demonstrated his resilience and perseverance while building with the large blocks in the garden.

> **Creating and Thinking Critically – thinking**
>
> - Having their own ideas.
> - Making links.
> - Choosing ways to do things.
>
> Xavier often has ideas and thinks creatively to solve a problem – for example, when he was building outside and a suitable block could not be found, Xavier thought of using the plastic steps as a seat in his car. He has a tendency to rush into things and finds it difficult if others do not want to do things his way. Xavier is learning to understand cause and effect, and notice patterns in his learning – for example, he saw the X-shape on the trim-trail ropes and said, 'X for Xavier!'

At the time of writing, the EYFS is under review. However, changes to the aspects and areas of learning do not change accepted best practice, with formative assessment at the forefront and moderation discussions to support summative judgements.

Moderation is a crucial component of the EYFS profile which ensures consistency of judgements and reliability of data. Each school will moderate their own judgements internally and will also be involved

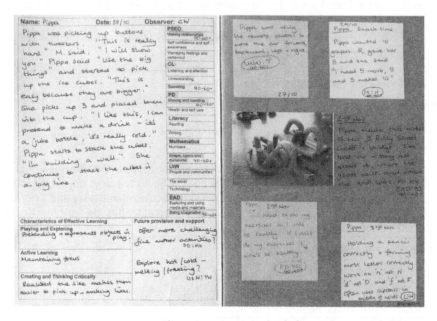

Figure 8.1   An example of observations recorded in an EYFS profile

with external moderation processes that look at a sample of profiles and encourage discussion around judgements made. This often involves schools meeting together to share profiles and discuss judgements made, and sometimes involves a moderator from the local authority visiting an individual school. The DfE provides exemplification materials to assist with moderation processes. Case study 8.1 describes one school's approach to EYFS moderation.

CASE STUDY 8.1 MODERATION IN THE EARLY YEARS

Katherine Bate, teacher at a primary school in Manchester

I teach in a large three-form entry primary school which has a very diverse intake of pupils, with a high proportion of children who have English as a second language. The relationship between teaching staff in parallel classes is strong, meeting together once a week to plan for the following week, using the children's interests. When it comes to moderation processes, both the class teacher and TA have a good idea of where the children started and we build on our baseline assessments throughout the year.

We do our own baseline assessments and home visits at the start of the year, which form the basis of our assessment over the year. Half of each class have attended our school Nursery class and had a home visit as part of their nursery induction. The other half have a home visit as part of the Reception induction. These visits are so worthwhile and really helpful, not only for safeguarding purposes, but also to help break down any potential barriers that may exist between home and school. In my current class, I have 13 children with EAL and the home visits for these children were invaluable. I visited with my teaching assistant and we built strong relationships with children in class based on these interactions and feel that we have a better understanding of their home and family.

Moderation is whole team and the EYFS team in school discuss individual children and their progress together. Our borough arranges moderation events throughout the year when teachers bring evidence and share this with other teachers and moderators. This is an opportunity to discuss individual children and ask for advice or guidance, as well as agreeing judgements together. Other teachers can ask questions and you can ask them questions - e.g. 'This child is borderline - what do you think?' In addition to these meetings, a moderator from the borough visits a proportion of schools each year. We need to ensure that we have evidence for all children covering all areas of learning and development so that we are ready to talk about and justify our judgements with moderators, senior managers, Ofsted Inspectors, etc.

The sorts of evidence that we collect to demonstrate progress and to share at moderation events include learning journeys, pieces of work, photographs, pic-collages of photos, long and short observations. We ensure that all areas of learning and development are covered over time and we can talk extensively about each child. We attach stickers with age-bands - e.g. 40-60 months, 30-50 months - to pieces of work or photos to demonstrate progress too. Although we share this evidence for moderation purposes, it is mainly used to help us to plan appropriately for our children, assessing formatively throughout the year. We do not do anything additional purely for moderation purposes. When moderating with other schools, I have found it most useful to share evidence with similar schools - not just local schools that may have a very different intake, but those with a similar ethos in Early Years.

(Continued)

(Continued)

Within our school, we also moderate across the classes, with Nursery and Key Stage 1 colleagues. It is important for us to know where children are going in their learning and for the Year 1 teachers to know where the children are, as well as for nursery colleagues to see where children progress to. We also have opportunities for other teachers within the school and senior managers to moderate at different points throughout the year.

WRITING MODERATION

In England, end of Key Stage teacher assessments of writing are moderated, with schools receiving external visits from local authority representatives at least every four years (STA, 2018a). Samples of independent writing are compared with exemplification materials and the Teacher Assessment framework statements (STA, 2018b) to ensure accurate and consistent judgements in line with national standards; an example of such statements is provided in Table 8.3.

Table 8.3   Examples of Key Stage 2 writing statements from the Teacher Assessment framework (STA, 2018b)

Working towards the expected standard	Working at the expected standard	Working at greater depth
The pupil can: write for a range of purposes.	The pupil can: write effectively for a range of purposes and audiences, selecting language that shows good awareness of the reader (e.g. the use of the first person in a diary; direct address in instructions and persuasive writing).	The pupil can: write effectively for a range of purposes and audiences, selecting the appropriate form and drawing independently on what they have read as models for their own writing (e.g. literary language, characterisation, structure).

Making judgements using the 'pupil can' statements in isolation is difficult, since there can be many different interpretations of, for example, 'effectively' or 'range'. Exemplification and moderation discussions are therefore essential when making such judgements.

An alternative way of moderating judgements is called 'comparative judgement', which is growing in popularity for complex tasks such as writing assessments, where a tick list of objectives can sometimes lose the sense and importance of the whole. 'Comparative judgement' or 'pairs comparison' is a method of assessment whereby two pieces of work are compared side-by-side and the teacher judges which one is better. By many teachers completing many online pairs comparisons, the results can be collated to give each piece of work a ranking on a scale. The judgement is holistic, so good for complex work like story-writing, where a list of criteria may not capture the essence of a successful piece. At the time of writing, comparative judgement is gaining traction, with organisations such as No More Marking (www.nomoremarking.com) providing online platforms for comparing work across the country.

SCIENCE MODERATION

There is no statutory moderation of primary science in England, but there is in Wales, where teachers meet in school and in clusters to compare judgements at the end of the Foundation Phase (age 7) and Key Stage 2 (age 11). Table 8.4 describes some approaches to moderation at three schools in Wales (Earle et al., 2018).

Table 8.4   Examples of science moderation in Wales

School	Examples of moderation practices
Tongwynlais Primary, Cardiff	Staff meet during INSET to moderate science work. Portfolios of work are produced to give staff examples of what different levels look like. Portfolios can also be shared at cluster moderations, which can help develop shared understanding of what progression in skills looks like.
Edwardsville Primary, Merthyr Tydfil	In Year 2, a piece of work is assessed each half term to identify which enquiry skills have been achieved and which need further practice. In Key Stage 2 teachers collaboratively moderate three pieces of work to agree standards of a higher, a middle and a lower attainment.
Year 5, Garnteg Primary, Pontypool	Teachers work in pairs to moderate pupil work, identifying features of the work that indicate the meeting of Welsh National Curriculum levels and identifying next steps. More than one pair look at each piece of work. The levels awarded are discussed and agreed; any discrepancies are discussed and resolved.

Where meetings take place throughout the year, there is an opportunity for moderation discussions to feed back into teaching and learning activities. Cluster meetings may include a representative from the secondary school to support transition, extending the understanding of progression. In Wales, similar meetings take place in other core subjects, but such a well-established moderation system takes time to develop. Queensland in Australia and Ontario in Canada also have long histories of consensus moderation, where *through discussion and debate, a shared understanding of standards is negotiated* (Klenowski and Wyatt-Smith, 2014, p75). For those countries that do not have such embedded systems of moderation practices, a simple starting point could be a 'graffiti wall' activity, described in Case study 8.2.

CASE STUDY 8.2   SCIENCE 'GRAFFITI WALL' MODERATION

An approach that has become popular through the Teacher Assessment in Primary Science (TAPS) project is called 'graffiti wall' moderation. Staff lay out examples on pupil outcomes in year group order along a roll of wallpaper or a line of tables and look at the range. The focus might be to look for progression in enquiry skills – for example, in the recording of results or drawing conclusions. Alternatively, when schools are trying this for the first time, a broader focus on the kind of science activities taking place might be appropriate. The aim of the graffiti wall is not in terms of standardisation, but is focused more on professional learning around progression.

(Continued)

(Continued)

For example, when work was laid out in one junior school, the teachers realised that providing a pre-printed table every time results were recorded meant that the pupils had not had the chance to learn how to draw a table of their own. Developing independence in Working Scientifically was also noted as a next step at Worlebury St Paul's Primary School in Weston-super-Mare, when they looked at three pieces of work from each year group (Earle et al., 2015).

Such sharing of pupil outcomes can also happen across schools, at cluster or network meetings. For example, when first tried at a South Gloucestershire network meeting, we found it hard to look at progression in Working Scientifically, because there was little evidence of science investigations (the work laid out was concept focused). So the group decided to try a similar investigation in their different year groups and bring the results to the next meeting. The cluster investigation was 'hand-span grab' (in Year 2 of the TAPS Focused Assessment database), a pattern-seeking enquiry where the children investigate whether bigger hands can grab more cubes. By carrying out the same investigation, the group saved time at the moderation meeting because they did not need to explain many different activities to each other. The activity was not narrowed to be recorded in a particular way, allowing all year groups to choose something appropriate for their pupils. Those attending the meeting who taught young children focused on drawing around hands and collating the results on to a class graph, while older classes focused on measuring hand spans and recording results in tables (Figure 8.2).

Many schools have gone through a similar process, whereby they take a single focus (like predictions or conclusions) or a single investigation (like rocket mice or craters) and bring together the pupil outcomes in a moderation graffiti wall as a starting point for professional learning.

Figure 8.2   Science moderation discussions supported by laying out work in a moderation graffiti wall

MODERATION FOR PROFESSIONAL LEARNING

As described above, moderation can be an opportunity for professional learning as well as standardisation of pupil outcomes. Opening up the discussion helps to develop confidence and expertise in assessment. Social moderation is *a participatory process that respects the professionalism of teachers as assessors who meet to consult one another in considering the judgements and to achieve consensus on the standards or grades awarded* (Connolly et al., 2012, p597). In considering the judgements and standards, teachers build a better understanding of their interpretation and application of criteria, and ultimately of the subject and the progression of concepts and skills within it. Better understanding of criteria and progression help teachers to devise teaching and learning opportunities that can provide appropriate challenge or support.

Klenowski and Wyatt-Smith (2014) describe how consensus moderation can support both the consistency of assessment judgements and improve teacher practice, with moderation discussions and disagreements: *generating new knowledge and understanding regarding interpretation of the standards* (p74). Moderation can help to 'calibrate' judgements and expectations. By comparing and discussing a selection of pupil outcomes, teachers can reflect on their practice and whether they are providing sufficient opportunities for the pupils to demonstrate the expected standard.

The kind of tasks that provide the pupil outcomes for moderation are a little in the 'Goldilocks' zone, in that they need to be 'just right' to stimulate fruitful discussion – focused enough, but not too narrow. For example, a cloze-the-gap activity would provide little information about individual attainment, while a long-term research project that could be presented in any way, would be hard to compare. There needs to be a balance between uniformity and diversity (Black et al., 2011, p462), since some uniformity is needed for moderation so that the comparison is between similar things, but the task needs to be open-ended enough to allow for diversity in outcomes.

There are opportunities for subject leaders to carry out moderation as part of their monitoring processes. The purpose of a 'book look' is to get a sense of what is happening in the subject in different year groups – for example, with a focus on progression in a particular area. It is essential that the results of such monitoring are fed back to staff thoughtfully, because the aim is to begin a dialogue about supporting learning, rather than prompt staff to defend their practice. Such monitoring is only a small step for moderation, perhaps to help decide areas of focus for future development. For moderation to make the most impact on professional learning, it should be a 'shared enterprise' (Klenowski and Wyatt-Smith, 2014, p2).

CONCLUSION

In this chapter, moderation has been defined as an activity which is broader than standardisation since it can be a key way of supporting assessment literacy in the teaching profession. *Moderated teacher assessment has been proven to facilitate staff development and effective pedagogic practice* (Green and Oates, 2009, p238). Discussions about pupil outcomes can support the development of *communities of practice* (Grant, 2013). Such discussions can range from informal comparison of a lesson with a colleague to whole staff meetings or a moderation graffiti wall, to comparison of work across a cluster or subject, as in 'comparative assessment'. How rigorous the debate is regarding the standards will depend on the use of the assessment, with higher stakes activities needing closer scrutiny and adherence to criteria. Moderation can be more productive for professional learning where assessments are not high stakes, since there can be more open discussions of the meaning of criteria and how to show progression in the subject at different ages.

REFERENCES

Black, P, Harrison, C, Hodgen, J, Marshall, B and Serret, N (2011) Can teachers' summative assessments produce dependable results and also enhance classroom learning? *Assessment in Education: Principles, Policy and Practice, 18*(4): 451–69.

Connolly, S, Klenowski, V and Wyatt-Smith, C (2012) Moderation and consistency of teacher judgement: teachers' views. *British Educational Research Journal, 38*(4): 593–614.

Davis, A (1998) *The Limits of Educational Assessment.* Oxford: Blackwell.

Department for Education (2017) *Statutory Framework for the Early Years Foundation Stage.* London: DfE.

Earle, S, Davies, D, McMahon, K, Collier, C, Howe, A and Digby, R (2015) *Introducing the TAPS Pyramid Model* (interactive pdf). Bristol: Primary Science Teaching Trust.

Earle, S, Jones, B, Coakley, R, Fenn, L and Davies, D (2018) *The Teacher Assessment in Primary Science (TAPS) Pyramid Model: TAPS Cymru: Examples from Wales.* Bristol: Primary Science Teaching Trust.

Grant, L (2013) Cross sectoral moderation as a means of promoting communities of practice. *The International Journal of Learning, 18*(12): 65–75.

Green, S and Oates, T (2009) Considering the alternatives to national assessment arrangements in England: possibilities and opportunities. *Educational Research, 51*(2): 229–45.

Harlen, W (2007) *Assessment of Learning.* London: SAGE.

Isaacs, T, Zara, C and Herbert, G with Coombs, S and Smith, C (2013) *Key Concepts in Educational Assessment.* London: SAGE.

Johnson, S (2013) On the reliability of high stakes teacher assessment. *Research Papers in Education, 28*(1): 91–105.

Klenowski, V and Wyatt-Smith, C (2014) *Assessment for Education.* London: SAGE.

Standards and Teaching Agency (STA) (2018a) *Assessment and Reporting Arrangements (ARA).* London: STA.

Standards and Teaching Agency (STA) (2018b) *Teacher Assessment Frameworks at the End of Key Stage 2.* London: STA.

Stobart, G (2009) Determining validity in national curriculum assessments. *Educational Research, 51*(2): 161–79.

9

CONCLUSION

SARAH EARLE

┌─── **PURPOSE OF THIS CHAPTER** ────────────────────────────────────┐

In this chapter we will:

- summarise the key messages presented in this book;

- explore the perspectives of different stakeholders in assessment;

- consider the implications of principled assessment for primary school practice.

└───┘

KEY MESSAGES

A number of other key themes regarding the principles and practice of assessment in primary schools have arisen throughout this book.

- Assessment is part of teaching and learning.

- Assessment can be used by pupils and teachers.

- Consideration of assessment purposes is important.

- Assessment practice can be evaluated using the key principles of validity and reliability.

- Whether an assessment is formative or summative depends on its use.

- Effective use of assessment also depends on understanding progression in different subjects/ phases.

- It is important to build assessment literacy in the profession.

Each key message is discussed further in turn below.

ASSESSMENT IS PART OF TEACHING AND LEARNING

This book has argued that assessment in the primary school is broader than what is generally assumed as the stereotypical assessment: the end of the topic test. Assessment is a key part of the teaching and learning cycle, within and beyond the lesson. Experienced teachers constantly use assessment information to tweak and adapt their lessons. If your question is met with a sea of blank faces, then you might rephrase it, or go back some steps, or reconsider the focus for that section of the lesson. This ongoing elicitation, judgement and evaluation is what makes teaching so dynamic and so exciting: every interaction can change the course of the lesson. As trainee teachers, it takes time to develop these skills, moving from *reflection on action* to *reflection in action* (Schön, 1983).

Development of assessment practice is more than employing a range of strategies; it is also about knowing what to do next, whether to use that information immediately or make a mental note of it as something to return to in a later lesson. Sometimes, the revealed misconception is directly relevant to the topic at hand and can be addressed immediately; at other times, it is related to a different area and needs to wait until later; alternatively, it may be an indication of a more deep-seated misunderstanding that will need some careful thought about what to do in the next lesson. The opposite can also occur: that a child's explanation can be surprising, demonstrating a more in-depth understanding than expected, which merits further discussion or a swap to a more challenging activity. By recognising assessment as part of teaching and learning, it can be used more effectively to support pupil learning.

ASSESSMENT CAN BE USED BY PUPILS AND TEACHERS

This book argues that assessment can be 'reclaimed' for pupils and teachers. Assessment should not be something that is 'done to' the child or teacher, as a passive recipient. The pupil should be active in the sense that they know how the activity will inform their learning journey. The teacher should be active in that they feel empowered to make principled decisions about the assessment practice in their classroom, armed with the knowledge that assessment should be purposeful. The assessment-literate teacher will recognise the need to balance the demands of accountability with the needs of their class, perhaps noting that using assessment information diagnostically will support data for accountability in the long run.

CONSIDERATION OF ASSESSMENT PURPOSES IS IMPORTANT

An assessment can only be judged as appropriate or useful if we know its purpose. Thus, it is essential to step back and consider what the assessment is aiming to do. For example, the aim could be to find out initial pupil ideas on animal classification to help plan the next lessons; to check what pupils have remembered from last week's lesson on the Ancient Greeks; to self-assess confidence with a particular maths strategy; or to decide on an overall grade for English. Each purpose has a different amount of content to be checked and a different level of implications. Some assessments may be immediately useful to the pupil or teacher; others require moderation to ensure reliability of judgements. Adoption of new assessment strategies should be the result of decision-making which considers whether implementing the innovation could lead to enhanced outcomes for pupils.

ASSESSMENT PRACTICE CAN BE EVALUATED USING THE KEY PRINCIPLES OF VALIDITY AND RELIABILITY

Once the purpose of the assessment is clear, its appropriateness and effectiveness can then be considered with reference to the key principles of validity and reliability. Some questions to support this are presented in Table 9.1. Manageability is also a concern when evaluating assessment practice, so the time taken to complete and analyse assessments should be considered in terms of whether there is sufficient impact on pupil learning to justify the time spent.

Table 9.1   Questions for starting to evaluate assessments

Purpose	Validity questions	Reliability questions
All	Does the assessment focus on the specific part it is supposed to?	Does the judgement draw on a shared understanding of progression in the subject?
Formative use by the pupil	Does the pupil know the focus for the assessment?	Does the pupil understand the criteria for success?
Formative use by the teacher	Does the assessment provide fruitful information about the focus? What should happen next?	What evidence is there to make the judgement?
Summative snapshot activity	Does the assessment provide access to the focus?	Is there consistency/agreement in the judgement criteria?
Summative summary	Have a range of areas and types of activity been taken into account?	Would other teachers agree with the assessment judgement?

WHETHER AN ASSESSMENT IS FORMATIVE OR SUMMATIVE DEPENDS ON ITS USE

An activity is not inherently formative or summative; such categorisation depends on the use to which it is put. Any assessment activity can be used for formative or summative purposes. For example, a topic test could be used summatively to judge recall within the unit, or formatively to plan the areas for focus in the final lessons of term. The majority of assessment activities should have a formative purpose, because this is more likely to support future learning. If assessment activities are for reporting purposes only, then it may be worth considering whether that is the best use of time in the primary school.

EFFECTIVE USE OF ASSESSMENT ALSO DEPENDS ON UNDERSTANDING PROGRESSION IN DIFFERENT SUBJECTS/PHASES

In order to make effective use of ongoing assessment, an understanding of progression is essential. By this we do not mean the tracking of pupil 'flight paths', but that there should be an understanding of the subject and what it looks like to get better at it. Generally in the primary school, pupils move from less to more independent, from using less to more vocabulary, from concrete to abstract, from simple to complex explanations, and so on. The National Curriculum gives an indication of the way subject-specific knowledge and skills can be developed across key stages, but this is often in general terms, so it is worth looking at exemplification from subject associations or more experienced colleagues to see what this looks like in practice. We are not assuming here that all children will develop understanding in the same way or at the same rate, but recognise that it is useful for teachers and pupils to know what they are aiming for: 'what a good one looks like'. Of course, more than one 'example' is essential, since you would not hold up a particular story as the one to aim for and expect carbon copies of the story written in pupils' books. The aim is to see the kind of thing that is expected, together with a variety of outcomes and possibilities.

If the use of assessment is only 'visible' in certain parts of the curriculum, then the message to the pupils is that only those parts of the curriculum are the parts that matter. Assessment can drive the curriculum for both the teachers and the pupils. If there is a strong focus on summative assessment for particular strands, the message is that it is these strands are important, that this kind of knowledge is valued (Edwards, 2013). By broadening the use of assessment to include an emphasis on formative practices, the knowledge and skills in any lesson can be valued, where the pupils seek to improve their map reading, their model making, their singing, their ball skills, and so on. An understanding of the progression of knowledge and skills across the curriculum supports the use of such formative practices.

IT IS IMPORTANT TO BUILD ASSESSMENT LITERACY IN THE PROFESSION

This book has argued that an understanding of assessment can be empowering for teachers and school leaders. Such an understanding, also called assessment literacy, is necessary to be able to make decisions about assessment practice at all levels of the school. Black et al. (2011) found that teachers needed to first recognise that change in assessment practice was necessary; this was accomplished by considering the validity of current practices. They found that assessment competence involved a combination of literacy, skills and values (p452) and for this the development of moderation was key. Klenowski and Wyatt-Smith (2014, p2) assert that assessment literacy includes the ability to design quality assessments, as well as the ability to use criteria and evidence to make judgements. They go on to describe assessment as a *shared enterprise*, with teachers having a central role in assessment reform (Klenowski and Wyatt-Smith, 2014). Such a shared enterprise involves the whole profession, which includes a wide range of stakeholders, as discussed in the next section.

STAKEHOLDERS IN ASSESSMENT

Different stakeholders in education, such as those listed below, will approach assessment with different perceptions of its purpose and how it should be enacted in the primary classroom. Each stakeholder is considered in turn, to support appreciation of both the different viewpoints of assessment, but also of the multitude of uses to which it is put (Mansell et al., 2009).

PUPILS

For pupils, assessment can be seen as 'high stakes', ranking against others in the class or country, or it can be seen as a 'low-stakes' everyday part of lessons. Which viewpoint is dominant is dependent on the classroom and school culture around assessment. It is all too easy to pass on the pressures of school accountability to the child. However, very few (if any) assessments at primary school need to be seen as 'high stakes' for the children. If the school processes require grading or ranking of some kind, this can be in the teacher's paper or electronic markbook, rather than on the pupils' work. As discussed in Chapter 3, comment-only feedback, which is a 'recipe for action' (Wiliam, 2018), will do more to support learning than grades or scores. This does not mean that children are not made aware of errors in their work – for example, in times tables or spelling tests – but that these test scores are 'low stakes', providing quick feedback about which spellings or tables to revisit – part of learning and retrieval practice, rather than 'high-stakes' summative assessments.

PARENTS

Parents are concerned about whether their child is 'doing OK' and are likely to see assessment as a means of ranking. Conversations with parents will often include discussions about data, but should also include more descriptive markers of attainment and next steps. For example, discussion could be based around a piece of the child's writing, noting their successes and next steps. Embedded formative assessment can be pointed out, to draw attention to the ongoing nature of assessment and how it is used to develop their child's learning – for example, with focused learning objectives, success criteria and self-assessment. For those children with additional needs, parents may want to discuss arrangements for accessing assessment activities.

TEACHERS

DeLuca and Johnson (2017) suggested that teachers and trainees are largely unprepared for developing assessment in their practice, and that learning to assess *involves actively integrating and practising assessment principles within their own professional learning so that they become intimately familiar with assessment processes and how they operate to support learning* (p125). It has been argued above that assessment is a key part of teaching and learning. Assessment should form part of the planning of every lesson, with consideration given to the most appropriate ways in which to know whether the pupils have 'got it' or not. It is also useful to consider the purpose of the assessment at the planning stage, to think about whether the information or evidence is likely to be used formatively, within or in preparation for the next lesson; or whether it will be used summatively to note attainment at a particular point in time. Teachers are responsible for this day-to-day planning and use of assessment information, together with their own classroom climate. With such a large amount of control over the selection and implementation of assessment strategies, it is essential for teachers to understand the purposes and principles of effective assessment practices.

TEACHING ASSISTANTS

A Teaching Assistant (TA) or Learning Support Assistant (LSA) is a valuable resource in the classroom, since they can not only provide tailored support for groups and individuals, but they can also be an extra pair of eyes and ears in the collection of assessment evidence. For instance, a TA can scribe a child's utterances in a floorbook, providing a record of their ideas, which can be used formatively or summatively. However, it is essential that the discussion of assessment purposes extends to the TA, so that they are clear about the purpose of the activity. For example, if the TA believes that task completion is the goal, then they will support all children to complete the required work, resulting often in similar outcomes, which have had wildly different amounts of input, while if the TA believes the task is to find out what the children know independently (as in a test situation), then they may offer no help or guidance at all. Therefore, the teacher who has planned the lesson needs to explain the purpose of the activity to the TA, which is often somewhere in between the extremes of 'task completion' and 'test situation'. As a teacher, it is useful to know how independently the children take part in the activity, but it is also usually a situation where scaffolding is appropriate to support the learning experience.

SENIOR LEADERSHIP

Senior leaders are one step removed from the classroom, but still responsible for what happens there. This means that senior leaders rely on a range of evidence when deciding on the most effective use of support and budgets. Numerical data is only one kind of evidence and it may be necessary for senior leaders to consider how valid and reliable such information is, if it is not based on standardised metrics. As discussed in Chapters 6 and 7, pupil progress meetings may be the time in which to discuss the performance of individuals and groups within the class. It is important to remember that such discussions will be more valid if a wide range of information is taken into account, so teachers should bring pupil books in for discussion, as well as summaries of attainment. Data may flag up points of interest, but closer examination is necessary to determine the 'story' behind the number. It cannot be assumed that linear progression or pre-decided 'flight paths' represent 'normal' progress. Outcomes are the result of a complex interaction between the pupil and the task, with extrinsic (e.g. amount of breakfast eaten, appearance of snow or a squirrel, etc.) and intrinsic (e.g. wording or context of the task) factors all playing a part. High expectations should be in place for all children, but this does not mean grading expectations or formula-based predictions; it means high expectations of pupil engagement in learning and progress as evidenced in books or in discussions with pupils.

GOVERNORS OR TRUSTEES

School governors or trustees are even further removed from the classroom and rely on teachers and senior leaders to provide them with assessment information. Also, governors are not usually trained teachers, so will need explanations of assessment terminology. Teachers and senior leaders will need to explain how assessment can only ever be an approximation of 'what is in the child's head'. That valid summative assessments of subjects need to take into account a range of information; that children do not all mature at the same rate (and that month of birth can have a big impact, especially in the Early Years); and that formative assessment can impact positively on pupil learning – all of this means that data summaries provided for governors need to come with an explanation regarding assessment processes and discussion of confidence levels in the data presented. Classroom visits may be recommended as a way for governors to find out about the practice in the school that sits 'behind' the numbers on the data report.

INSPECTORS

At the time of writing, a consultation for a new Ofsted inspection framework for England is underway (Ofsted, 2019), which suggests that there may be less focus on data in the future. School data will still act as a trigger or a signpost, but it will not be taken as the whole story – not the 'be-all and end-all' (Harford, 2018). The draft handbook suggests instead a focus on intent, implementation and impact of the curriculum, and notes the importance of developing understanding of assessment.

When used effectively, assessment helps pupils to embed knowledge and use it fluently, and assists teachers in producing clear next steps for pupils. However, assessment is too often carried out in a way that creates unnecessary burdens for staff and pupils. It is therefore important that leaders and teachers understand its limitations and avoid misuse and overuse.

(Ofsted, 2019, p44)

Each stakeholder may come with a different viewpoint about the uses of assessment, but all stakeholders need to understand assessment practices and the principles behind them. This may involve the school or teachers communicating with different stakeholders individually or as a group. Those who are furthest from the classroom may need examples of pupil activities and outcomes to help them understand principled assessment practice.

PRINCIPLED ASSESSMENT

In this book, we have argued that teachers and schools can make decisions about assessment practices within and beyond the classroom, and to help them to do that we asked them to consider the principles of purpose, validity, reliability and manageability. Assessment guidance and practice appears to be rapidly changing, but the same questions can be asked by teachers or school leaders about any assessment.

- What is the purpose of the assessment? (What will the outcomes be used for?)

- Is it valid? (Does it assess what it is meant to?)

- Is it reliable? (Are the results sufficiently trustworthy for the purpose?)

- Is it manageable? (Is this an efficient use of time?)

By asking such questions, the teacher is developing their assessment literacy, their understanding of assessment and its application. However, the teacher does not stand alone; they are part of a wider school community that may need to work together to develop a shared understanding of assessment. They may consider whether the assessment practices that have evolved over time are all fruitful in terms of the amount of effort and time they take, compared with their impact on pupil learning. Such development of a shared understanding of assessment, a shared assessment literacy, is a developmental process, mediated by context and school culture (DeLuca et al., 2016, p264).

Assessment can be an active and dynamic process, with the child at the centre. If this does not describe the assessment practices in your class or school, then we direct you to the questions above, to evaluate those practices and decide whether they are fit for purpose.

REFERENCES

Black, P, Harrison, C, Hodgen, J, Marshall, B and Serret, N (2011) Can teachers' summative assessments produce dependable results and also enhance classroom learning? *Assessment in Education: Principles, Policy and Practice, 18*(4): 451–69.

DeLuca, C and Johnson, S (2017) Developing assessment capable teachers in this age of accountability. *Assessment in Education: Principles, Policy & Practice, 24*(2): 121–6.

DeLuca, C, LaPointe-McEwan, D and Luhanga, U (2016) Approaches to classroom assessment inventory: a new instrument to support teacher assessment literacy. *Educational Assessment, 21*(4): 248–66.

Edwards, F (2013) Quality assessment by science teachers: five focus areas. *Science Education International, 24*(2): 212–26.

Harford, S (2018) Ofsted blog: schools, early years, further education and skills. April. *Assessment – what are inspectors looking at?* Available online at: https://educationinspection.blog.gov.uk/2018/04/23/assessment-what-are-inspectors-looking-at/

Klenowski, V and Wyatt-Smith, C (2014) *Assessment for Education: Standards, Judgement and Moderation.* London: SAGE.

Mansell, W, James, M and the Assessment Reform Group (2009) *Assessment in Schools: Fit for Purpose?* London: Teaching and Learning Research Programme.

Ofsted (2019) *School Inspection Handbook: Draft for Consultation – January 2019.* London: Ofsted.

Schön, D (1983) *The Reflective Practitioner: How Professionals Think in Action.* London: Temple Smith.

Wiliam, D (2018) *Embedded Formative Assessment* (2nd edn). Bloomington, IN: Solution Tree Press.

INDEX

Added to a page number 'f' denotes a figure and 't' denotes a table.

ability, assessment and 14
accountability 1
  assessment for 5, 10, 47, 51, 56
  balancing the needs of the class with 98
  career development and 51, 74
  data-driven 74, 83–4
  definition 78t
  measures 83
  need for assessment literacy 88
  pupil progress and 58
achievement
  defined 13
  distinguished from progress and attainment 60–1
  mutual construction of 34
Active Learning (motivation) 89–90t
age-related expectations (AREs) 5, 9, 21, 58
  examples 59–60t
age-related goals (ARGs) 58
analogies 38t
art
  challenging the notion of linear progression
    (case study) 66–8
  sketchbooks as records of assessment 51–2
assessment
  awareness of preconceived ideas 88
  comparative judgement 92
  conflicted position of teachers 5
  in context 5–6
  data see data; data analysis
  defined 9
  development of practice 98
  effective use dependent on understanding
    progression 99–100
  evaluation 98–9
  functions and effects 5
  importance of understanding 2–5
  key messages 97
  key terminology 8–17
  non-statutory 2, 65
  paradigm shift 5
  as a political issue 5
  principled 13–16, 103
  of pupils with SEND 69
  purposes, consideration of 98
  reforms 5
  shared understanding 15, 16, 103

  stakeholders in 100–3
  tasks, as evidence of progress 66t
  teachers' standards 3–4t, 5
  teaching, learning and assessment
    cycle 2–3, 97–8
  as value-laden 5
  see also formative assessment; summative
    assessments; teacher assessment
assessment criteria 15
  in peer and self-assessment 36–7, 41, 44
  in summative assessments 48, 51
  teacher assessment 88
Assessment for Learning (AfL) 10
  see also formative assessment
Assessment of Learning (AoL) 10
assessment literacy 3, 5, 16, 88, 98, 100, 103
Assessment Reform Group (ARG) 10
attainment
  defined 78t
  distinction between progress and 59, 60–1
  in England 11–13
attainment targets 75t
  examples 59–60t
Austin's butterfly 42
autonomy (pupil) 34

baseline testing 65, 69
'best fit' judgements 49
bias(es) 48, 88
Black, P. 10, 19, 100
Boaler, J. 33–4
book look 95

career development, and accountability 51, 74
challenge
  assessment for calibrating level of 20t
  pupil choice in level of 28
Challenge Advisers 73, 81–2
Characteristics of Effective Learning 89–90t
child-level data analysis 80f
children see pupils
choice, in level of challenge 28
clarity
  of assessment criteria 44
  on purpose of assessment 36, 41
  on purpose of questioning 42

Clarke, S. 27, 28
class-level data analysis 80f
classroom activities, moderation based on 88–9
classroom culture 2, 42, 43, 44
closed elicitation 23
cluster meetings 93, 94
co-construction 33, 42
coaching 29–30
coasting standard 83
collaborative learning 21, 34
comment marking 30, 100–1
commentaries, summative assessments 51
Commission on Assessment without Levels
    (2015) 5, 47, 76t
communities of practice 95
comparative judgement 15, 49, 92
comparison, assessment for 5, 12
computer-based assessment (CBA) 11
consensus moderation 93, 95
consequences of assessment 49
consolidation of learning 37
construct under-representation 14, 16
construct validity 14
construct-irrelevance 14, 16
constructive feedback 36, 42, 43, 63
content validity 14, 16
context-free learning intentions 27–8
context-specific learning intentions 28
convergent activities 23
conversations, as evidence of progress 66t
Council for the Curriculum, Examinations and
    Assessment (CCEA) 11
Cowie, B. 34, 42
Creating and Thinking Critically 90t
creative assessments 51–2
criteria
  for moderation 87
  see also assessment criteria; success criteria
criteria compliance 15
criterion-referenced assessment 9, 12, 15, 49, 75t
cross-school moderation 89
curriculum, assessment for monitoring/
    reviewing 51

data
  defined 77t
  as driving force for school improvement 73
  frequency of collection (data drops) 1
  generation, in primary schools 73
  growing importance of 74–5
  international comparison of 5
  as more than a set of numbers 76
  Ofsted use of 83–4
  use of IT for creating and tracking 52
data analysis
  different levels 80–2

key definitions 76–7, 77–8t
key questions for 81f
possible actions resulting from 81t
school self-evaluation (case study) 82–3
see also tracking
Dearing Review (1994) 75t
DeLuca, C. 3, 101
delving questions 25t
Department for Education (DfE) 3t, 83, 91
dependability 15
desired learning outcomes 21, 22f
diagnostic assessment 10, 11
dialogue 10, 23–4, 24–5t, 42, 67, 87, 95
divergent activities 23

Early Learning Goals (ELGs) 53t
Early Years Foundation Stage (EYFS)
  summative assessments 51–2
  tracking progression (case study) 70–1
  see also Foundation Stage Profile (FSP)
Education Reform Act (1988) 75t
elicitation 22–3
empowerment (pupil) 31, 34
empowerment (teacher) 98, 100
End of Key Stage assessments (SATs) 47,
    49, 50t, 65, 69, 74, 75t
End of Key Stage expectations 65t
England
  assessment descriptors 3t
  attainment and progress 11–13
  changes to National Curriculum (1988-2015) 75–6t
  concerns about reliability of writing
      assessments 15
  Early Learning Goals (ELGs) 53t
  English and maths summative assessment 51
  responsibility to promote pupil progress 63
  school performance tables 62
English
  indicators of pupil progress 59t
  summative assessment 51
English as an additional language (EAL) 71
evaluative assessment 11
Every Child Matters (2003) 13
evidence
  assessment as collecting and interpreting 9
  of pupil progress 65–6
excellence, sharing examples of 21t
exemplification 49, 87t, 91, 92, 99
'expected' levels of progress 60
external reliability 15
extrinsic motivation 42

feedback
  assessment and provision of 10, 20t
  comment-only 100–1
  effective 29–31

as evidence of progress 66t
prompts for pupils' written 36
pupil progress in relation to 64t
replacing marking with (case study) 30
see also constructive feedback; peer feedback
feedback policies 1
feedback sandwich 37t, 38
Filer, A. 15
Final Report on the Commission on Assessment with Levels (2015) 13
fixed intelligence 14
floor standard 83
floorbooks, using (case study) 70–1
focused assessment 23
formative assessment 2, 19–31
    impact on learning 102
    as learner support 5, 10
    link between pupil progress and 19
    pupils' use of 33–44
        assumptions about pupils' skills 43–4
        pupils' perceptions of their role 41
        see also peer assessment; self-assessment
    purpose of 10
    shared understanding of criteria 15
    teachers' perceptions 10–11
    teachers' use of 19–31
        as bridge between teaching and learning 31
        importance 20–2
        strategies 10, 22–31
    validity 14
Foundation Stage Profile (FSP) 50t, 52, 54
    Early Learning Goals (ELGs) 53t
    moderation 89–92
'four corners' activity 38t

gaps analysis 20t, 21, 60, 63, 64t, 66t
General Teaching Council for Northern Ireland 4t
General Teaching Council for Scotland 4t
geography, indicators of pupil progress 59–60t
government, monitoring pupil progress 62
governors 62, 102
grades, assessment in form of 10
'graffiti wall' moderation (case study) 93–4
group discussion 31
group dynamics 36
group moderation 88
groupings, in peer assessment 36, 42

'hand signals' strategy 37t
Harford, S. 58–9
Harlen, W. 15–16, 47, 48, 78, 84
Hattie, J. 21, 27
high achievement 60
high expectations 102
high quality assessment 3, 23
high stakes assessment 10, 11, 46, 47, 74, 88, 100

hinge questions 24t
holistic judgement 92

improvement
    mutual construction of 34
    use of data to drive and sustain 82
independence (pupil) 34
independent peer assessment 43
Independent Review of the Primary Curriculum: Final Report (Rose Review) 76t
information technology (IT) 52
Inside the Black Box 19
Inspection Data Summary Reports (IDSRs) 83
instrumental understanding 26
inter-rater reliability 15, 87
interactions, as assessment 9
interactive element, of formative assessment 36
interdependence 36
internal reliability 14–15
international comparison 5
intrinsic motivation 42
invalid assessments, avoiding 14
ipsative judgement 9, 12, 15

Johnson, S. 3, 101
judgement(s)
    assessment as 9
    based on attainments and progress 12
    'best fit' 49
    comparative 15, 49, 92
    DfE and Ofsted 83–4
    holistic 92
    inter-rater reliability 15
    moderation and consistency and calibration of 88, 95
    personal bias in 48
    'secure fit' 49
    teachers' summary 10

Key Stage-level data analysis 80f
Klenowski, V. 3, 95, 100

labelling 5
language
    learning intentions and success criteria 28
    see also shared language
leadership teams
    approach to pupil progress 61–2
    as stakeholders in assessment 102
league tables 51, 84
Leahy, S. 24
learning
    assessment criteria and consolidation of 37
    assessment to support 5, 10, 20t, 102
    characteristics of effective 89–90t
    relational view of 41

self-view and engagement in 42
summative assessment and design of future 47
see also teaching, learning and assessment cycle
learning intentions, and success criteria 27–9
learning journeys 21, 98
learning objectives
    pupil progress in relation to 63–4t
    We are learning to (WALT) 39
'learning walk' activity 38t
lesson evaluation 63t
lesson planning
    assessment as part of 101
    explaining to TAs 101–2
lessons, questioning during 24
level descriptors
    removal of 5
    school attempts to recreate 6
linear progression, challenging the notion of 102
    (case study) 66–8
low achievement 60
low attainment 69
low stakes assessment 100
Lum, G. 5

McIntosh, J. 13, 47, 49
McKay, D. 51, 74
manageability 16, 98–9
Mansell, W. 15
marking
    as evidence of progress 66t
    feedback in the form of 30
    policies as feedback policies 1
    providing time for children to respond to 20t
    pupil progress in relation to 64t
    replacing with feedback (case study) 30
    see also moderation; standardisation; triple
        marking
maths conferencing (case study) 25–7
maths summative assessment 51
maximum validity 15
Messick, S. 14
metacognition 34
mid-lesson plenaries 21t, 29, 30
misconceptions, addressing 20t, 22, 23, 25t, 26,
    27, 98
'mock' tests 14
modelling 35–6, 42
moderation 15, 86–9
    criteria for 87
    examples 87t
        Foundation Stage Profile 89–92
        science moderation 93–4
        writing moderation 92
    exemplification materials 91
    focus for 87
    meetings 48, 93, 94

outcomes for 87, 95
process of 87
for professional learning 49, 94–5
of summaries of learning, Northern Ireland 10
moderators 87
motivation 42
multiple criteria 36

narrative, assessment in form of 10
National Curriculum 49, 50, 51, 99
    changes to (1988-2015) 75–6t
National Foundation for Educational Research
    (NFER) test 69
national-level data analysis 80f
No More Marking 92
non-statutory assessments 2, 65
norm-referenced assessment 9, 12, 15
Northern Ireland
    assessment descriptors 4t
    assessment terms 11
    responsibility to promote pupil progress 63
    summaries of learning 10

objectivity 15
Ofsted 11, 13
    focus on pupil progress 62
    School Inspection Handbook 13
    as stakeholders in assessment 102–3
    use of school data 83–4
The Ofsted Inspection – Clarification for Schools 13
online data tracking systems 65
open elicitation 23
open questions 24t
optimal reliability 15
oral rehearsal 23
outcomes
    attainment and achievement used to describe 13
    evaluative assessment 11
    feedback through exploring examples 31
    for moderation 87, 95
    see also desired learning outcomes
ownership 25t, 31, 34, 37, 63t, 71

pairing, in peer assessment 36, 42
pairs comparison *see* comparative judgement
paradigm shift 5
parents
    monitoring pupil progress 62
    as stakeholders in assessment 101
peer assessment
    in action (case study) 40
    as an interactive process 33–4
    children's perceptions of their role in
        (case study) 41
    classroom culture and questioning 42–3
    designing activities 34–7

for providing feedback 31
  strategies 37–8t
peer checking 37t
peer dialogue 42
peer feedback
  Austin's butterfly 42
  ownership and engagement 37
  strategies 37–8t
phonics screening 50t
planning
  peer and self-assessment activities 34–5
  questioning 23, 42
  summative assessment to support 47
  using formative assessment to inform 20–2
Playing and Exploring (engagement) 89t
plenary buddies 38t
Pollard, A. 15
preconceived ideas 88
predictive validity 14
'present and ask' activity 38t
Prior, J. 23
prior learning
  assessment of 21, 22f
  connecting new learning to 20t
  questioning to activate 23, 24
'process or procedural' criteria 28
'product or outcome' criteria 28
professional learning, moderation for 49, 94–5
progress
  defined 78t
  Ofsted measures 83
  see also pupil progress
progression
  challenging the notion of linear 102
    (case study) 66–8
  effective use of assessment dependent on
    understanding of 99–100
  example of tracking in the early years (case
    study) 70–1
  moderation and shared understanding of 86
  for pupils with SEND 68–9
prompts, for children's written feedback 36
psychological safety 36
'pupil can' statements 92
pupil conferencing 25
  maths conferencing (case study) 25–6
pupil progress
  and accountability 58
  assessment linked to 5, 19, 20t
  for children with SEN (case study) 69
  defined 58–9
  distinction between attainment, achievement
    and 60–1
  England 11–13
  ensuring and supporting 63, 63–5t
  evidencing 65–6

'expected' levels of 60
indicators of
  English example 59t
  geography example 59–60t
lack of 69
measurement 65
meetings 102
monitoring
  stakeholders involved in 61–2
  through summative assessment 47, 51
  tracking see tracking
Pupil Progress Reviews (PPRs) 78–9
  case study 79–80
pupils
  as active participants in assessment 33, 34, 98
    see also formative assessment
  choice in level of challenge 28
  giving time and opportunity to devise/pose
    questions 21t, 24, 25t
  needs, consideration of 63t
  as stakeholders in assessment 100–1

Qualifications and Curriculum Authority
    (QCA) 74
quality assurance 88
quality control 88
questioning, in assessment 10, 23–4, 24–5t, 42–3
questions, writing learning intentions as 29

reflection 98
relational view of learning 41
reliability
  balancing validity and 15–16
  defined 14–15
  moderation and 86, 88
  questions for evaluating 99t
  summative assessment 48–9
  teacher assessment 16
reports 51
respect 36, 42, 43
Rose Review (2008) 76t
Rowe, M.B. 23

sampling 14
scaffolding 35, 43
school culture 2, 103
school inspectors see Ofsted
school performance tables 62
school reports 51
school self-evaluation (case study) 82–3
school-based assessment 47
school-level data analysis 80f
schools
  assessment for ranking 10
  external pressures on 84
  use of summative assessments 51

science moderation 93–4
Scotland
    assessment descriptors 4t
    responsibility to promote pupil progress 63
'secure fit' judgements 49
self-assessment
    as an interactive process 33–4
    children's perceptions of their role in
        (case study) 41
    designing activities 34–40
    as part of the lesson (case study) 39
    for providing feedback 31
    strategies 37–8t
self-regulation 34
self-review, traffic lights for 37t
self-view (children's) 42
senior leadership see leadership teams
shared language 48, 49
shared understanding 11–12, 15, 16,
    42, 54, 86, 103
Shaw Primary School (case study) 40
Skemp, R. 26
sketchbooks
    as records of assessment 51–2
    to support pupil progress (case study) 66–8
snapshot assessments 10, 48
social construction of responses, giving pupils
        time for 23
social moderation 95
social pressures 36
social relations 42
software packages 52, 77
special educational needs and disabilities (SEND),
        progression for pupils with 68–9
Special Educational Needs (SEN) Code of
        Practice 69
'spot the mistake(s)' questions 24t
staff development, moderated teacher
        assessment 95
stakeholders
    approach to pupil progress 61–2
    in assessment 100–3
Stanbridge Primary School (case study) 69
standardisation 15, 48, 87–8
statements
    success criteria 28
    summative assessments 49, 52
statutory assessment tests see End of Key Stage
assessments (SATs)
stepping stones, pupil progress as 59–60t
Stobart, G. 14
Stoberry Park Primary School (case study) 39
subject knowledge (pupil) 21t
subject knowledge (teacher) 27
success criteria
    collaboration

in achievement of commonly agreed 21
    in evaluation of outcomes against 21t
    learning intentions and 27–9
    pupil progress in relation to 63–4t
    What I'm looking for (WILF) 39
summaries of learning 10, 51
summative assessments 2, 46–56
    for accountability 47, 51, 56
    at transition 52–6
    between the ages of 2 and 11 49, 50t
    commentaries 51
    consequences of 49
    early years see Foundation Stage Profile (FSP)
    importance for teachers 46–7
    as more than testing 47–8
    negative perception of 5
    non-statutory 65
    pupils with SEND 69
    purpose 10, 47
    reliability 15–16, 48–9
    shared understanding of criteria 15
    teachers' perceptions 10–11
    types 48–9
    validity 48, 102
    within and beyond the classroom 50–2

target setting
    assessment for 10
    culture of numerical 74–5
    pupil progress in relation to 64t
Task Group on Assessment and Testing (TGAT) 5
teacher assessment 75t, 88
    balancing of reliability and validity 15–16
    moderated 95
Teacher Assessment Framework 49, 92
Teacher Assessment in Primary Science (TAPS) 23,
        54, 55f, 93
teacher knowledge 27
teachers
    career development and accountability 51, 74
    conflicted position of 5
    monitoring of pupil progress 61
    perceptions of assessment 10–11
    as stakeholders in assessment 101
    use of assessment 98
        see also formative assessment; summative
            assessments
teachers' standards 3–4t, 5, 63, 68
teaching
    learning and assessment cycle 2–3, 97–8
    using formative assessment to inform 20–1t
teaching assistants 101–2
terminology 8–17
tests/testing 10, 14, 47, 65
'think, pair, share' 38t
thinking questions 25t

'3-2-1-Go' 38t
'thumbs ups, thumbs down' 37t
'tick box' culture 15
Torrance, H. 23
tracking
    by senior leadership teams 61–2
    definition 77t
    online 65
    progression in the early years (case study) 70–1
    reasons for 78–9
    software 52, 77
'trade-off', between reliability and validity 15
'traffic lights' strategies 37t, 38t
transferable skills 43
transition, summative assessment at
    case studies 54–6
    Early Years Foundation Stage Profile 52, 53t
triple marking 1
trust 36, 37, 41, 42, 43
trustees 62, 102
'two stars and a wish' 37t, 38
2-2½ years' review 49, 50t

validity
    balancing reliability and 15–16
    defined 14

moderation and 88
questions for evaluating 99t
summative assessment 48, 102
teacher assessment 16
value laden, assessment as 5
visible learning 21–2

wait time 23
Wales
    assessment descriptors 4t
    Challenge Advisers 73
    responsibility to promote pupil
        progress 63
    science moderation 93
We are learning to (WALT) 39
Wedell, K. 69
Welsh Government 4t
What I'm looking for (WILF) 39
Whitestone Primary School (case study) 82–3
whole-class mini-plenaries 30
Wiliam, D. 10, 15, 19, 27
William, D. 24, 31
word choice, learning intentions and success
        criteria 28
writing moderation 92
Wyatt-Smith, C. 3, 95, 100

KEY
MESSAGES

- ☐ ASSESSMENT IS PART OF TEACHING AND LEARNING.
- ☐ ASSESSMENT CAN BE USED BY PUPILS AND TEACHERS.
- ☐ CONSIDERATION OF ASSESSMENT PURPOSES IS IMPORTANT.
- ☐ ASSESSMENT PRACTICE CAN BE EVALUATED USING THE KEY PRINCIPLES OF VALIDITY AND RELIABILITY.
- ☐ WHETHER AN ASSESSMENT IS FORMATIVE OR SUMMATIVE DEPENDS ON ITS USE.
- ☐ EFFECTIVE USE OF ASSESSMENT ALSO DEPENDS ON UNDERSTANDING PROGRESSION IN DIFFERENT SUBJECTS/PHASES.
- ☐ IT IS IMPORTANT TO BUILD ASSESSMENT LITERACY IN THE PROFESSION.